How To Get To The Top Of Google

Tim Kitchen
Head Ninja, Exposure Ninja
www.ExposureNinja.com

Free Website and Marketing Review with Customised Strategic Plan worth £186+VAT for readers at www.ExposureNinja.com/Google

Contents

Introduction

The first time I helped someone else's business get to the top of Google I was hooked. From promoting my own businesses I knew what Google ranking meant in terms of traffic, sales and perceived authority. But helping other people made it more real.

To hear him speak you'd swear he had just won the lottery or got back from a Tony Robbins gig. His confidence, self-assurance and *pride* were in a different league from when I'd left him. He'd always been a nice guy, but from kicking around the house he shared with his mum all day, wondering when the next job would come in, to *this* was something even I hadn't expected. I tried to interview him but he wouldn't let me get a word in edgeways.

Ben was my first freelance client purely because he was the only tradesman in the sleepy Devon town (Tiverton) I was living in that was desperate enough to agree to be my guinea pig. Lucky for him it didn't turn out too badly, and in two months he went from nowhere to being the most visible plasterer in town, thanks to the basic Wordpress template website I built and promoted for him. A dead basic site built with the Kreera theme (I think I even downloaded a cracked version) that I built in 3 hours to test my theories had *changed his life completely*. His partner was able to reduce her work hours so they could spend more time together and he was in a position to start thinking about buying a house. He couldn't stop saying thank you, and for the first time I saw what getting a website to the top of Google *actually* meant to people like Ben.

My name is Tim and over the last 9 years, I've been the guy that businesses of all shapes and sizes call when they want more exposure for their website. In that time, my company and I have helped over 1,900 businesses in every imaginable market, in all corners of the world through our training, consultancy and 'done for you' online marketing.

We've had some spectacular results (many of which I'll be breaking down step by step for you in this book), and made a lot of businesses a *lot* of money in the process.

This book is where I lift the lid on exactly what we do to achieve these results, so that you can copy the same techniques for your own business. It's a completely open account of *exactly* what it takes to boost a website's ranking on Google, and there are plenty of other exposure and profit-boosting tips in here too. Straight up, loud and proud: the goal of this book is to show you how to make more money from your website.

More visibility, more traffic, more customers - that's it. By the way, the goal isn't to tell you how awesome Exposure Ninja is or highlight the inadequacies of a previous SEO company you might have used. If you want *that*, give us a ring or visit our website instead.

Who is this book for?

This isn't like any other SEO book. For one, it doesn't even have SEO in the title. But more about that later... This book isn't for geeks or experienced SEOs; it's primarily for the following groups of people:

- Business owners & entrepreneurs
- Employees in charge of their company's Internet presence (marketing directors, managers or assistants).
- Search Engine Optimisation (SEO) companies – both existing companies and freelancers thinking of starting their own SEO Company.
- Bloggers and hobbyists who want to improve their website visibility and get more traffic.

In short, if you want to get a website to the top of Google, this book will give you a step-by-step guide to do it.

Prominent Google ranking really can make or break a business, so while the tone is generally light hearted and conversational (there's enough boring SEO stuff out there already) that shouldn't distract you from the importance of what we're doing here.

You will find some simple fundamental rules that many business owners are breaking *without even knowing it,* which doom their websites to obscurity. You'll probably notice that some of your competitors are making these mistakes right now, and you may even spot a few in your own business. You'll learn some small tweaks that can send your ranking shooting up, and you'll begin to identify some of the hidden SEO 'anchors' responsible for holding your site down.

Whether you plan to do your own SEO or hire an outside company, if you rely on the Internet for business growth you HAVE to understand as much about SEO as possible, to help you make the choices that are best for your business. With the relationship between prominent search engine ranking and business success, understanding how this world works should be one of your top marketing priorities. Ignorance in this field is like an athlete that doesn't understand the basics of nutrition. Your business *cannot* perform well online without getting this stuff right.

The good news is that in this book we'll break everything down into clear steps with plain English explanations. These are the very same strategies that companies around the world pay huge sums for with one good reason: they work.

I hope you are excited by the possibilities and I look forward to hearing your success story!

Google's Panda & Penguin Updates

The world of SEO has changed so dramatically in the last few years that the companies at the top of their game in 2012 are almost all fighting for their lives, if they're not already bankrupt. Google's ranking algorithm updates in 2012 began penalising websites that were using a brand of promotion strategy considered manipulative and unnatural. The so called 'Penguin' updates starting in April 2012 were the final nails in the coffin for many of the most widespread SEO techniques in use by those looking for fast and cheap results. Fear and panic spread through the industry as website rankings plummeted and many online businesses began to worry if their livelihoods were at stake now that many of their bread and butter strategies were not only ineffective but actually *harmed* rankings. Literally overnight entire businesses were wiped out and if you think I'm exaggerating you should read the sob stories. I'll include some later on for you if you're that way inclined (because they're instructive not because you're intrigued by the pain of others, of course).

We'll be looking at the effects of Penguin, Hummingbird and other Google updates throughout this book, as there are lessons to be learnt and pitfalls to be avoided. The good news is that the basics have never changed, and it's possible to execute a 'future proof' strategy by sticking within Google's guidelines without sacrificing excellent results.

If your site's ranking has been harmed by a Google update, keep reading as we'll be covering in detail how you can begin the recovery process.

Why this book exists

This book exists for two reasons: firstly, I noticed that there were a lot of businesses out there that didn't want 'done for you' help with their SEO, but clearly DID need to do something. The existing information about DIY SEO is, on the whole, ineffective and hopelessly vague. Attending conferences, watching popular SEO YouTube channels and checking out blogs gives very little enlightenment to the amateur marketer about what they're actually supposed to do, while everyone just beats endlessly on about what they're *not* supposed to do. As a result, the DIY'ers have been losing ground to the big spenders and a class division was emerging.

In short, Google has started becoming like the Yellow Pages used to be: the big companies with huge marketing budgets can afford to get top positions, whereas smaller businesses were forced onto page 2 or worse. And of course if you're not on the first page, you're invisible.

Once they were forced off page 1, their business dropped and they began to struggle. It's a vicious cycle that ends very badly for those who don't (or can't) pay to compete.

The second reason I decided to write this book is another frustration about the SEO industry: It seems that the majority of businesses entering into the world of paid SEO have absolutely no idea how to judge a good company from a bad one, and without understanding what is involved in promoting and optimising websites, they really have no way of judging good quality SEO from spam. They buy the wrong service to save a bit of money and end up spending two years completely invisible as they try to recover from Google penalties.

We spend about 20% of our time helping companies who have made a poor SEO choice to correct the damage of this work, and it's extremely frustrating for the business owner who has to pay us to fix work they thought *was* the fix!

Worse still are those businesses that have been hit so hard by ranking penalties that their sites are unrecoverable. A while back I did some consultation with a lovely couple that ran a niche information site and made their living from the Advertising revenue. Unfortunately, they used a junk SEO Company to promote the site that simply spammed blog comments and spun junk articles. A couple years later the site was hit so heavily by a Penguin update that penalty recovery was impossible. They battled it for a year before calling it quits and closing the site. It was a real shame considering the once active forum and the huge volume of original content they created. The site was their livelihood and she ended up having to get various jobs writing freelance.

Hopefully the tips in this book will prevent you from making a similar mistake when it comes to choosing a promotion partner.

The 3 'Dirty Secrets' SEO Companies Don't Want You To Know

1. Many SEO companies are primarily sales organisations. The person you talk to on the phone understands only what their Sales Manager has told them about SEO. If in doubt, get a second opinion. And if it sounds too good to be true, *I promise you* it is. Anyone that promises you a ranking in a specific time period is lying, point blank. If you'd like a free second opinion I'm also happy to help - drop me an email to tim@exposureninja.com but please be patient for a reply!

2. You understand your market and your customers better than any SEO company can. Therefore you are a huge SEO asset to your business. You're well placed best placed to identify what your audience wants, where they hang out online, and what it is about you that appeals to them. You are actually very well positioned to oversee the marketing of

your website, so taking the time to learn the basics is extremely important. Any SEO company that doesn't involve you is doing work that is too generic to be any use.

3. Many 'SEO Companies' actually don't do any SEO, and are simply lead generation call centre companies that outsource the whole lot and charge you a fat commission. With the information in this book, you will be able to translate what they tell you and see past the salesmanship. Next time someone tries to pitch you for SEO services, you'll be well placed to judge for yourself whether or not what they are offering is worth the fee. Search for my video 'How Good is Your SEO Company' to get my top tips in avoiding the scum.

Cheap SEO

In our experience, the vast majority of cheap SEO is a total waste of time and you'd be better off going it alone. Since low quality 'spam SEO' stopped being effective, companies charging very small fees are so restricted in the work they can actually afford to do, they either continue using the spam tactics they always used or, more commonly, no longer do any work at all!

We see a lot of SEO reports as clients send us info from their previous SEO companies to analyse. This makes for very interesting reading! The majority of cheap SEO reports contain so many graphs and statistics (all automatically generated), that the client fails to notice that there isn't a single paragraph in the report that mentions the work that was actually carried out that month. Embarrassingly what customers are paying for is actually just an automatically generated report, tracking normal ranking fluctuations. With SEO, you really do get what you pay for and unfortunately if what you're paying seems too good to be true, it almost certainly is!

In Spring 2014 we started working with an e-commerce client who happened to send over a report that their previous SEO Company had sent them. The whole thing was a rebranded print out from a popular SEO tool, and it was immediately clear that the company had done absolutely no work to earn their sizeable monthly fee. But what shocked me most was that the figurehead of the company was one of the most respected figures in the SEO world. Perhaps one of the top 15 authorities in the world.

For what it's worth, companies of all sizes and experience levels fall for the same tricks again and again. In an industry in such desperate need of regulation, make sure that you tread carefully and fully trust whoever you're doing business with.

The Minefield

By now you might be getting the impression that the world of SEO is inhabited mainly by low life scoundrels and call centre sharks. While it's true that most of the inhabitants of SEOville could have been kicked out of the used car sales forecourt for their tactics, the huge potential of prominent Google ranking mean that a new line of contestants is always lined up ready to take their turn to try and stumble through the minefield to the riches awaiting on the other side.

When you get it right however, SEO is extremely profitable. Throughout this book I'll be giving my tips for finding a suitable partner if you decide not to go it alone.

How Level a Playing Field is Google?

One of the most exciting things about the Internet (and Google in particular) is that it is supposed to offer a level playing field: every business competes on the same Google results page, regardless of the company size or age. When it works properly, consumers have a genuine choice.

I'm a firm believer that this is how it should be - a meritocracy with each player having the same chance to win. What it *shouldn't* be is a high-entry fee auction where the big players get bigger and the smaller fish starve to death.

There's a richness to search results that include recognisable brands alongside hidden gems and innovative newer businesses. Audiences appreciate the speed and convenience of Amazon, but that doesn't mean that alternatives can't thrive as well. Boutiques and department stores can happily coexist online and consumers appreciate the choice.

So how close does this ideal match with reality?

The days when websites 'accidentally' ranked highly are over. For any search with *commercial intent*, the top rankers are paying for that ranking, either through an SEO agency or by the time spent doing it themselves. It's certainly possible for smaller sites to compete with the big players, but they have to give the task its proper priority. Setting aside a day or £200 each month to compete with Amazon in the search results is like turning up to fight Sparta with a broom handle.

The key to competing, winning and *dominating* in this environment is keeping your web strategy bang up to date and give it the proper importance. Those who promote their websites most effectively will win, no matter their company size. Would securing a stream of customers to your business be worth spending an hour per day on? And yet many businesses who tell you they're ambitious give their website promotion a spot at the bottom of their priority list. Do nothing and you'll get nothing.

I'm here to help you with your online marketing by showing you everything you need to do to compete online - however large or small you are, experienced or brand new. We've done this hundreds of times in every imaginable market and I'll lay it out, step-by-step, for you to copy.

How to use this book

There's no way around the fact that there is a lot of information in this book. Some of the tips, tricks and strategies in this book represent years of research and take many hours (even *months*) to implement. Others are quick and easy tricks you can do today to get fast results.

My advice is to cherry pick the strategies that suit you. Do the ones which are most relevant to you and which fit in with the time you have available. But please bear one thing in mind:

If spending a lot of time on a certain task turns you off, you are not alone. Your competitors are thinking the exact same thing. That's why they're not doing it. And that's why you should.

It boils down to how much you really want this and if you are willing to invest the time and effort necessary. By reading this book you are off to a very good start.

I would recommend that you read about each and every strategy, whether you plan to implement it or not. It's helpful to know about the tools in your arsenal, even if you don't intend to use them. You'll start to spot these techniques in action, and you may find yourself looking at the Internet in a very different way! Prepare to become a geek.

If you are a freelance Search Engine Optimiser or run an SEO company, you'll want to know it all. Should you find yourself working with a client in a particularly competitive niche it will be helpful to have some 'heavy firepower' to back you up and give you the edge against the competition.

If you are a small business and your competitors are employing a dedicated SEO company, you will be forced to do more work to compete (for advice on how to check what your competitors are up to, read on).

But please understand that just because they are employing an expensive company doesn't mean you can't beat them. They are likely using the same techniques you will learn about in this book. With your specialist understanding of your market and your customers, you are actually in a competitive position. And remember: 'expensive' doesn't necessarily mean 'good' in the world of SEO (although it's a safe bet that 'cheap' does always mean 'bad'!).

The Structure of this Book

As the title of this book suggests, we will be focusing primarily on Google throughout, and we'll start by understanding how Google really works. The good news is that the strategies in this book work just as well for other search engines including Yahoo, Bing, Yandex, Baidu,

AOL (which uses Google search) and the hapless, dead in the water Ask.com.

In the Western world, the clear trend over the past decade is Google's increasing dominance while other search engines fight for smaller and smaller scraps. There is good reason for this, as Google is at the cutting edge of search technology and works extremely hard to make its search engine the most accurate and useful on the planet. In some markets Bing is stealing some ground but, on the whole, anything that works to boost Google ranking is even *more* effective on Bing so this is where we'll focus our attention.

A quick word about Google's updates: any updates that Google implements are to keep its position as number one and increase its market dominance. This is a GOOD THING for us, even though it might not feel like it at the time. There is no vacuum: each time there is a Google update, some websites are penalized while others subsequently receive a boost in rankings. There is simultaneous outcry and joy expressed across the world on Internet forums. As we will see later on, the best long-term tactic for good Google ranking is to be legitimate, honest and strictly above-board when optimizing and promoting our website. Google just wants the best for its end users (the searchers) so as long as we keep *the searchers* happy, Google will continue to reward us with good ranking.

After looking at Google, we will take a look at your own website and how to make it 'Google Friendly' as well as 'visitor friendly'. Always remember that your website is built to generate customers, leads or readers for you or your business. Never sacrifice that aim in order to get good Google ranking. Being at the top of Google won't happen if your website doesn't lead to more happy visitors, customers and profit for you.

The third section of the book looks at promoting your website around the Internet. This is absolutely crucial for high ranking and constitutes the majority of on-going work that you will need to do in order to get and maintain top position on Google.

Finally we will look at piecing together a strategy for your website's Google dominance. You will see examples of my own strategies for getting websites to the top and, as always, you are encouraged to 'swipe at will' and use for your own website.

For efficiency's sake, from now on I will be assuming that you are a business and the purpose of your website is to attract customers and make money. Whether you are an SEO company, SEO freelancer or you run an information website or blog, the principles are exactly the same.

You'll also notice throughout that I mention certain freebies to help you with your SEO.

These freebies include free expert reviews, information, video software and voucher codes. The more entrepreneurial readers will take advantage of as many of these freebies as possible, because some of them - our free expert SEO and website review, for example - can save you weeks or even months of trial and error and give you a distinct advantage against your competition.

This Book is Not Written By a Professional Author

I am not a professional author, I'm a professional website marketer. I write how I talk and when choosing between 'easy to understand' and 'fancy language' I'll always opt for the former. That means there will be times when those eagle-eyed readers might notice a grammar or spelling error. If you want an SEO book written by someone who has no experience in SEO but has far superior writing skills, I'd be more than happy to make a bucketful of recommendations.

I've set up, run, analysed, consulted with, and managed SEO for over 500 businesses over the past 9 years, from starting out building my own websites to setting up the UK's leading tradesman online marketing company and then, since 2012, running Exposure Ninja to build and promote sites for businesses around the world.

For each and every website I've owned, promoted and been involved with, getting prominent position on Google was absolutely critical to their success. Some of them were in markets that didn't previously exist, so getting to the top of Google was relatively easy and it was all about maintaining that position once the competition started flooding the market. Others fought fierce competition with established rivals and beating them in the 'Google Shootout' was a lot harder-fought and bloody.

You will see and hear about examples of both sorts throughout this book.

The end result is that I know what I'm talking about. For Exposure Ninja and I, first place on Google isn't a 'nice idea' or wish; it's a part of daily life.

I don't say this to brag, I just want you to know that this stuff comes from testing, measuring and experience, not reading the Moz blog everyday and blindly regurgitating it to anyone who will listen.

In this industry there are so many self-proclaimed 'experts' who have had little experience out on the front line. They cough up stories about strategies they've never implemented and offer opinions on topics they've only heard mentioned on forums. They're the sorts of people who proclaim to have the solution to the latest Google update within hours of it going live. My advice is to judge everyone by the results that their advice brings you.

And beware of the wizard.

Reader Offer: Free Expert SEO and Website Review

As a thank you for buying this book and to give you a head start as you embark on your plan for Google domination, I'd like to give you a little something: a completely free SEO and website review from Exposure Ninja, the Web and SEO company I run. To claim yours, head over to www.exposureninja.com/review

In your review one of our marketing experts will analyse your website, SEO and your presence on the web. We'll also take a look at what your competitors are up to, make a note of anything that they're doing particularly well and let you know about any opportunities that they might be missing. We'll email you our findings in a PDF file or talk them through in a walkthrough video. You'll also see an option to have me do your review personally.

The aim of the review is to give you a clear picture of where your website and online marketing stand at the moment and show you the areas you should focus on to get the best return in the shortest possible time.

Case Study: London AV Installation Company

It was late 2012 and I was running the largest tradesman marketing company in the UK after word had spread about Ben the Tiverton Plasterer's success online.

When I say 'word had spread', what I mean is that 'I had spread the word' by writing for all of the UK's leading magazines targeted at tradesmen telling them about the results we were getting for our plumbers, electricians, roofers and scaffolders. I then filmed DVDs showing the results because people didn't believe it, and sent thousands of these DVDs out around the country. Thus, word spread.

The techniques we were using to promote those sites had never been seen in these industries, so it was like turning up at a Sunday league football game with half of Real Madrid team on your team. We were just *dominant*. We were routinely hitting position one in a month, and in some uncompetitive rural areas we had some sites hitting top position *before they were even properly launched*. Others outranked well-established national companies, and we even had one site take up 6 of the first 7 Google results in its area. We had to produce DVDs showing the results, because our clients didn't always have computers and, unless they saw it with their own eyes, they didn't believe it was possible.

Word spread and eventually we started taking on larger clients in different industries, and eventually this grew into the monster that is Exposure Ninja.

One of EN's first clients was a supercool company in London run by a very entrepreneurial chap whose name I won't share (because his competitors would be very interested to see how they've managed to be so dominant on Google!). They install home cinemas amongst other things. Not just home cinema *equipment*, but *home cinemas*. So cool.

Anyway, we sat down and identified a huge number of searches that they wanted to rank prominently on Google for. The number of phrases was large - it was well over 50, and even I started to wonder if it was really going to be possible.

To explain how we did it, it helps to understand that Google rewards websites with a) lots of original, well-written descriptive text content and b) plenty of links, particularly if these links are from authority sites in the same industry.

Before we started building their new website we mapped out a website structure that had over *a hundred* pages targeting every brand, product and area they sold. Most of their established competitors' sites had around 20-30 pages before they were knocked off the top. All of a sudden Google noticed this *bible* of information appear with more text than all their competitors combined. To build the authority of the site we started listing them in every good quality local and market-relevant directory we could find. Then we started pitching Interior Design magazines and websites with well-written articles that matched the style of their publication. We offered them the articles free of charge, of course positioning our client as the writer of the article and getting a link back to our site.

Within a year and they were ranked on the first page for 41 of their target phrases, with position one for a whopping 20 different searches. Totally freakin' Ninja. You can be sure I cracked out a tub of Ben and Jerry's Peanut Butter Cup to celebrate that one.

Google

What Being at the Top Of Google Will Mean For Your Business

I don't need to tell you how important Google is, whether you're selling cars, tarot readings or last minute gifts.

When your customers look for your product or service, chances are that they use Google most of the time. In the UK, Google is the main search engine for 90% of the population. The rewards from prominent ranking are unlike any other lead source in existence. It's the equivalent of having the biggest boldest ad on the first page in the Yellow Pages.

For many businesses, being on the first page of Google is enough to sustain them with no other marketing activity. Enough prospective customers are out there looking for that product or service that just being found on Google is enough to feed a high-ranking business a steady stream of customers.

The *Principle of the Slight Edge* says that there are exponentially greater benefits for those who are first in their market, even if they're only first by a nose. The horse that wins the race by a nose wins 3 times as much as the horse that comes second by a nose. It didn't have to be three times faster, it only had to be a nose faster.

The Principle of the Slight Edge is alive and well on Google, with those on page one enjoying a disproportionate benefit compared to those on page 2 and beyond. But the slight edge applies even further *within page one*. The most recent figures suggest that the first 'organic' result of the first page in Google gets 38% of all the clicks on the page. Imagine siphoning off *38%* off all traffic searching for your target phrases before your competitors even get a chance to make their pitch!

Later on we'll look at more advanced strategies for dominating the Google results page, including the example where our client grabbed 6 of the first 7 results!

Having stressed the importance of first position, I also want to remind you that appearing *anywhere* on the first page is better than being lost in the dark depths of pages 2 and beyond (with one exception: a 2011 study showed that being ranked first on page 2 actually got more clicks than being ranked 10th on page 1. But that's the exception).

So in general page 1 equals good. Page 2 or worse equals bad.

Implied Expertise

Most of the general public don't understand what it takes to be first on Google, and actually this is a clue to why it works so well. If they knew that the sites were ranked according which website was best optimized and had the highest PageRank (we will look at PageRank later on), they might dig a little deeper.

Instead, many simply assume that the top result in Google is 'chosen' because it's the best and they place their trust in Google to serve them the best result. In general it works out, and that has built a behavioural habit.

The top result might have shoddy customer service, high prices, and be run by the mob - Google *doesn't care*. Or rather Google *has no way to track this* (yet). All Google does is run mathematical calculations (algorithms) based on thousands of different ranking factors, and out pops an ordered list of websites:

Ranking factors => Algorithm => Search Ranking

Change the variables, change the output. SEO is really that simple.

The 3 Ways to Show Up On Google's First Page

On Google there are 3 different places you can show up on the first page.

Most people tend to focus on the *organic* Google listings. These are the main results that show up in the wide left hand column. This area is called *organic* because it is not directly paid for. The sites are positioned there through a number of ranking factors, which we will look at in a minute.

The second way to show up on the front page of Google is through advertising. Google's Adwords program means that website owners can pay to show up above the organic results (marked with little 'Ad' icons) or down the right hand side of the page. This might seem like a nice shortcut to getting on the front page, but the vast majority of web surfers are conditioned to avoid adverts. So although these ads are shown right at the top of the page, combined they receive only around 20% of the clicks.

The third way to show up on the front page is for local searches, through Google+ Local listings, previously called Google Places. These results are shown on a map, and for mobile searches they tend to be even more prominent than on desktop. For many local searches, these map listings appear in amongst the traditional organic listings, pushing down some of the organic results. This emphasises the importance of being found not only high up in the organic results, but also prominently on the map. We'll be looking at how businesses with physical locations can *utterly dominate* their local map later on.

The Google Leapfrog – Using Video To Leapfrog Pages of Your Competitors

There's actually a fourth way to show up on the first page of Google, which is relatively under-used. Google will often show videos in search results if it decides they're relevant, and this can sometimes be an easy way to get fast prominent placement. Ranking promotional videos is a nice little trick that you can use to leapfrog pages and pages of your competitors, which we'll look at in the Third section of this book.

How Google Decides Where To Rank You

The big question: how does Google decide who to show at the top and who to show second?

The answer is in the complex and secret algorithms they use to measure, amongst other things:
- The site's relevance to the search
- The popularity and authority of the website across on the Internet
- The number of pages, products and amount of content on the site
- User experience, for example the number of broken links, missing pages and the bounce rate, which all harm ranking.

Relevance

More than anything, this is the word that defines Google's success to date. If the search results it served weren't the most *relevant* in the business, this book would be called How to Get to the Top of Lycos, because Google certainly wasn't the first in the market or the search engine with the best advertising. But its success has come from serving up consistently relevant results and a quick search on one of the other search engines (with the exception of AOL and others actually powered by Google) demonstrates how easy it is to take for granted the relevance of Google results.

SO HOW DOES GOOGLE MEASURE RELEVANCE?

There are a many factors that are used to measure relevance so let's briefly look at some of them now before drilling down in more detail later on throughout this book.

Top of the list is the content of your website. That is the words and, to some extent, the pictures. Google has software that is affectionately called 'robots' reading the Internet constantly. These robots are crawling over your website and making a note in the index every time each word appears. This process is called indexing. When someone carries out a search on Google, it runs through this index looking for instances of the words used in the search and coughs up the websites that they appear on.

Myth Buster: Indexing

Indexing does not mean 'saving' your entire website, and Google doesn't store your whole website, but rather instances of particular words and phrases.

Google also doesn't index every single page it finds. There are a huge number of web pages online that get no visitors and which Google doesn't bother indexing. It skips these pages because it prefers to prioritise the websites it considers more important, namely those that are being updated and getting more traffic. The bad news is that if your pages aren't indexed, they aren't going to be showing up in the search results. So getting indexed is a top priority and we'll look at ways to encourage Google to index your web pages later on.

Traffic

Websites that attract the most clicks from Google search results tend to move up in the rankings. Remember that Google wants to present the most relevant websites to its visitors so if lots of people click on site B even though it ranks below site A, then Google would see site B as being more relevant to its users and should move it up the rankings.

We know that Google measures the percentage of people that click on each of the advert shows (called the Click Through Rate, or CTR) and the CTR affects the position of these adverts. In the same way, CTR affects organic rankings too, so it makes sense to make your website's listing as appealing as possible (more on this later).

We also know that Google measures the 'bounce' from search results. If you Google "weather in Los Angeles" and click on a search result that doesn't give you this information, you're likely to quickly 'bounce' back to the search results, and choose a different result. Google sees this behaviour as a negative vote against the site, and is likely to affect its ranking if this behaviour is repeated by lots of people over time.

If the visitor bounces back to Google and amends their search, perhaps making it more targeted or modifying it in some way, this indicates that the search itself wasn't properly targeted enough and so won't affect ranking.

PageRank

PageRank is the secret sauce that Google uses to measure the relative popularity and authority of all the websites on the Internet. To understand *why* Google might want to do measure the relative popularity and authority of all of the sites on the Internet, imagine this highly improbable situation:

Due to a strange set of circumstances, you have to recommend a restaurant in a town that you've never been to, to someone that you *really want to impress*. If you make a good recommendation,

34

they'll like you forever. Make a bad recommendation and you're struck off their Christmas card list for good. The stakes couldn't be higher.

So how would you go about drawing up your list of recommended restaurants?
Well you might start by assuming that the restaurants with the longest queue outside are the most popular, so therefore would make a good recommendation. After all people wouldn't wait in a line to get into a mediocre restaurant. So the longer the line, the safer the bet. If you were really savvy, you might look for people waiting in the lines who are similar to your friend, indicating that *people like your friend* visit this restaurant.

In this analogy, measuring the line length is what Google's PageRank algorithm does online. But rather than *people stood in a line*, it measures links to each website.

If lots of links point to web page A, but no links point to web page B, then web page A usually has a higher PageRank. More links means that it's probably a more useful and popular page, so therefore it should be shown more prominently on Google. Incidentally the 'Page' in PageRank has nothing to do with the web*page* but is named after Larry Page, the supergeek Google co-founder who thought up the mathematical algorithm to measure it.

But it's not just the number of links pointing at a website that determine its PageRank. It's also the *quality* (and PageRank) of the websites that these links come from.

This makes total sense if we use a website example:

My website gets a link from spam blog comment on a website that gets no visitors, whereas your website gets a link from the Harvard University homepage (.edu website addresses hold particular weight with Google because they are less susceptible to being taken over by spammers). Which link means more? Obviously your link coming from a big authority institution holds far more weight.

This would be reflected in the subsequent PageRank that our websites get from the links. Your website would get lots of PageRank from the Harvard link, mine would get very little from the spam blog comment.

PageRank 'flows' through the links, so the Harvard website (which itself has high PageRank because so many other websites link to it) would pass PageRank to your site. The low quality blog that linked to my site would have much lower PageRank (no one links to rubbish websites), so would have less to pass on.

Note that just like head lice spreading through a primary school, giving another site PageRank doesn't mean that your site *loses* PageRank by linking to it. There's plenty to go around. But the PageRank a website passes on is shared between all of the outbound links on that page.

For example: let's say that your web page was the single solitary link from the Harvard homepage. In this highly unlikely example, your site would receive a *ton* of PageRank. Imagine Harvard saying, "This web page is the real deal. You have *got* to see this".

If on the other hand there were hundreds of links on the Harvard homepage and yours was only one of them, the PageRank that gets passed along would be shared by all the links on that page.

The only way to *create* PageRank is to create a new page. Each page is born with PageRank, and shares this PageRank with all the pages that it links to.

This means that bigger websites with more pages naturally have the opportunity to get a higher PageRank, because all their smaller pages feed back into the homepage and boost its authority.

We're going to be looking shortly at why you should build lots of pages on your website and what you should be filling them with, but for now think of lots of pages in orbit around your homepage all feeding PageRank to it.

Let's leave PageRank there. We'll briefly revisit it when we talk about links later on, but for now remember that PageRank is Google's measure of importance. And the PageRank of a page has a significant effect on where it shows up in the Google listings.

Keywords

We mentioned that Google's robots crawl your web pages and make a note of words that are found on them. When someone types in a phrase, Google scans its memory of the Internet for instances of that phrase.

The phrases people type into Google to find your products or services are called keywords. For example "plumber in London", "diet plans" or "how to get to the top of Google".

These keywords are extremely important when building and optimizing your website and you will become extremely familiar with your particular keywords by the time your website is top of Google. Every proper page of your website that is supposed to attract visitors (i.e. not privacy policy or the other 'boring' pages) should be built around - and optimized for - keywords relevant to the product or service it targets.

The keywords that you choose will depend on your business, your particular service or product, your competition and the habits of your customers. Remember that it's not just your homepage that can show in the search results, and in many cases your homepage actually isn't the ideal page for visitors to enter your site through. For that reason each of the pages on your site will target slightly different keywords, with some common keywords being used across all pages. This gives you a far broader range of phrases that your site can show up for than just your main money phrase.

Reader Offer: Free Lifetime updates to this book

Google is constantly moving the goal posts and as a result we are constantly adjusting, refining and adding new strategies as we experiment and find new approaches that work for ranking websites high on Google. I usually update this book a couple times a year to include these new strategies. If you would like to receive updated copies, free, for life, plus a summary of the new content each time, then head over to www.get2thetopofgoogle.com/offers

Picking Profitable Keywords

One of the most common SEO mistakes businesses make is targeting the wrong keywords. The first mistake is targeting only their business name: e.g. "ACME Scrap Metal" rather than the category "scrap metal companies" or even the problem their customers need solved "scrap metal removal". It's typical that in our marketing reviews we notice that a website owner is inadvertently telling Google that they only want to rank for their brand or company name.

Do potential new customers *really* search for your business specifically by your name? Do they even search for your product or service? Or do they search for what it *does* for them?

Let's look at an example: Pete runs Pete's Autos, a car mechanics in Croydon.

His regular customers might type in "Pete's Autos Croydon", but whether or not Pete's site targets this phrase aggressively, in most cases Google is going to show Pete's site for this search *anyway*. So Pete doesn't need to put too much effort into optimising his site to show up for this phrase and will be better off targeting more profitable phrases.

It's the customers typing in "car mechanic Croydon" or even "new BMW clutch Croydon" that represent extra new business for Pete, so

40

these are the keywords Pete should be writing on his list.

The first step in getting your website to the top of Google is sitting down with a pen and paper and drawing up a list of these potential target keywords. Start by listing all of your main products and services and add possible descriptions for each of them *in the language of your customers*. Pete's Mega Car Service Package might be "car servicing", "car service and valet", "car servicing local pickup" and "fast car servicing" for example.

Then under each of your products or services, identify the problems it solves and the benefits it provides, again, in the language of your customers.

If you're a local business, then it's worth specifying in your list the areas that you service. You'll want to think about how wide an area to cast, and you'll have to use your common sense here. For example a cake shop is likely to target an area of perhaps 4 square miles in a medium-density town. Visitors are unlikely to come and visit from much further afield than that, so targeting the town name and the specific districts around the shop will suffice, as typically searches will be made on a district basis ("cake shop Chelsea" rather than "cake shop London")

Photographers on the other hand are far less restricted geographically. Searches for photographers might use town or even countywide searches, so they would be wise to add the towns and counties that they travel to to their list.

By now you should have a big long list which we'll be fine tuning and running through some analysis tools to identify the best ones to target in the short, medium and long term.

Let's see what some of Pete's Keywords might be:
- Car mechanic
- Car repair
- New clutch
- Clutch repair
- MOT
- MOT test
- Fast MOT
- MOT while you wait
- MOT local pickup
- MOT retests
- Wheel alignment
- Car servicing
- Car servicing local pickup
- VW repair
- VW servicing
- Etc....

One thing to note is that the longer the phrase, the more specific the search. Generally the more specific the search is, the lower the competition and the easier you can rank for it. So if we're working with a brand new website we'll usually start by promoting for these 'longer tail' phrases ("car servicing local pickup") and start targeting the broader, higher competition phrases once the site has some authority.

In this example the phrase "local pickup" is what we call a *modifier*. Modifiers are words that can be added to your keyword or phrase that matches one of your benefits or advantages. For example "emergency", "24-hour", "local", "trusted", "free delivery" "next day delivery". By adding these modifiers to keywords on your page you can often pick up the 'low hanging fruit' and get good placement for particular long tail phrases that your competitors might be ignoring.

Analysing Your Keywords Using the Google Keyword Planner

Next, we're going to expand our keyword research by heading over to the Google Keyword Planner. To get the tool, simply Google "Keyword Planner" and click the link. You'll need to sign up for an Adwords account if you don't already have one.

This super ninja free tool from Google itself allows us to research exactly what people are searching for, how many people are searching for it, and searches related to it.

To begin with choose the 'Get Search Volume' option and drop in your list keywords and choose your location in the targeting section. If you're a nationwide business (e.g. E-commerce), choose your country. If you're a local business, add each of the towns or regions in your target audience.

What comes out is a graph showing an indication of total search volume by month over the previous year, along with average monthly search volume for each keyword. By clicking the dropdown menu at the top of the graph you can also see search volume comparison between desktop and mobile devices too, and typically this is in the region of 25 - 40%. Proof if you didn't already need it that your website needs to be mobile friendly! But more about that later.

If your target searches have low monthly search volume, this isn't necessarily cause for panic. We have seen fortunes made (albeit modest ones) by dominating lots of phrases indicated by Google to be low volume. The statistics aren't precise and it's more accurate to use the Keyword Planner to analyse *relative* rather than **absolute** search volumes.

How to Work Out Your Most Profitable Target Searches

The Keyword Planner also gives us some valuable insight into how profitable each phrase can be. The Competition level column indicates the volume of competition amongst advertisers for each phrase, and the Suggested Ad bid is an indication of how much they are willing to pay *per click* to advertise using Google ads. The higher the amount people are willing to pay, the more money they're making from that keyword. If you can get to the top of Google's organic listings for the phrase "New York Divorce Attorneys" for example, you'll make a lot of money: advertisers are willing to pay $70 *per click* to advertise to this traffic.

While we're here, I just want to touch on *commercial intent*. The phrases that lead to purchases rather than just information are said to have *higher commercial intent*. Consequently they lead to higher advertising spend, and are more profitable to rank for.

To illustrate, imagine the difference between somebody searching for "Digital Cameras" compared to someone searching for "Canon 70d free delivery". It's clear that the person searching for a specific camera with a modifier like "free delivery" is much more likely to make a purchase, as they're at the point of choosing a vendor that offers free delivery. By contrast the search for "digital cameras" could signal a variety of intentions: research about digital cameras, pictures of digital cameras, pictures taken by digital cameras, the history of digital cameras, or purchase of a digital camera. Only one of these can possibly result in money changing hands, so savvy advertisers avoid such broad phrases.

What if Google Would Suggest the Phrases You Should Target?

Who better to ask about the best phrases to target than Google itself? To see Google's suggestions in the Keyword Planner, click the Modify Search button and choose *Search for new Keyword and Ad Group Ideas*. As well as putting in the keywords you've identified, you can tell Google your website address and area of business. It will then give you a list of keywords that it thinks could be relevant based on the search habits of Google users and targeting by advertisers.

How to Choose Your Short, Medium and Long Term Keywords

Once you have your list of keywords, we're going to break them into 3 categories: short/medium term keywords, long-term keywords and everything else.

If you're already ranking well for the more specific keywords on your list, then you'll want to start targeting some of the more general phrases. In this case your *short/medium term keywords* will be those broader phrases closest to the phrases you're already ranking well for.

If your site is new or not yet ranking prominently for any searches, you'll want to start off by targeting some of the lower competition and more specific phrases, perhaps around some of your bestselling products and services rather than the business itself (e.g. "LED light cube" rather than "LED light shop")

Long-term keywords will be the very broadest in your list, provided they have adequate commercial intent.

Everything else will be a phrase with low commercial intent ("LEDs") or those that are so competitive that it's not realistic to expect prominent ranking (say, for example, that you sold books about the Amazon Rainforest. "Amazon books" might be one such unrealistic phrase!)

Analysing Your Competition & Identifying their Strengths and Weaknesses

Now that you have your list of target keywords, it's time to analyse your competition. When we're talking about SEO competitors, we don't necessarily mean *business* competitors, but the websites you are up against in your target searches on Google. It's not unusual for a business to give us a list of their competitors to find that, actually, the guys stealing all their traffic online are a completely different list of companies.

It's important to know what you're up against for a couple reasons:
1. Savvy competitors can save you work by showing you what you should be doing – all you need to do is copy them and do more of the same.
2. Less savvy competitors can highlight serious gaps in their approach that you can use to your advantage and leapfrog them in the Google rankings.

Let's start right at the beginning. Go to Google and search for the one keyword you would most like to rank for.

PRO TIP: Checking Ranking

To check your website's ranking as seen by everyone else, make sure you're using your browser's Private Browsing or Incognito mode. If you're signed into Google or using Google Chrome, the search results Google serves you will have been tailored to your search and browsing history. If you visit your own website a lot, it'll show far higher for your searches than it would for regular searcher, giving you a skewed impression of where you're really ranking. If you've just realised that your site ranks a lot lower than you thought, I'm sorry it was me that had to break this to you!

For the purpose of this exercise don't panic about where you show up, we're focusing on your competition here:
- Who is showing up at the top of the listings? Are they a direct competitor to your business?
- Who is second? And so on...
- Are any of your competitors are showing up more than once?
- Are there a lot of Google adverts for this keyword?
- Are any of your competitors using these adverts?
- Does Google suggest related searches at the bottom of the page? Should some of these be added to your keywords list?
- Are the sites that show up mostly directories or real businesses? Small businesses or large businesses?

If you are a local business, as well as the above:

- Is a map showing up in the search results?
- If so, how many map results are showing up?
- Is the map at the top of the search results, further down, or mixed in with the normal Google results?
- Do the map listings have a lot of reviews? When you click on their Google+ pages are they filled in and looking professional, or are they basic and generic with very little useful information?

Once you've absorbed all the information from this page, choose your second most desirable keyword.

- Does the same competitor show up in top position for this search?
- How many of the positions for this keyword are taken by competitors that showed up in the previous search?
- Are the same companies advertising as before?

I usually repeat this exercise with the 5 top keywords. The point of this is to really understand which companies are my main online competitions for Google's top spot. If five different websites are coming top for the keywords, that means we have a different competitor for each top spot, so we'll want to study each of their strategies for each keyword.

If one website is consistently in first place for all the keywords, it usually means they really know what they're doing and have put a lot of work into this. I say *usually* - if it's a small niche or very local area it could just be pure luck. Either way they're going to get a nasty surprise later on when we overtake them.

The next thing we do is identify 3 main online competitors. Again, we're not necessarily talking about businesses that compete directly with yours, but sites that we're competing with for ranking. They could be big chains or online retailers, or simply websites offering information.

If yours is a particularly commercial or competitive market, there will likely be more than 3 main competitors. If this is the case, pick the 3 biggest ones for now and write them down.

Of course, if your market is extremely uncompetitive or inhabited by technophobes it might be the case that you don't actually have 3 competitors online. In which case, be thankful and write as many as you have.

Deconstructing Your Competitors' Websites

We're now going to forensically study your competitors' websites and find out how they got to number one so we can beat them. Those readers that are uncomfortable with anything technical should skip to the next section if they find that they're struggling with any of the geekier competitor snooping!

Pick your number one competitor and search for the keyword that makes them rank highest. We're going to have a look at exactly what shows up in the search results. Notice the title of their listing on Google: does it contain the keyword you searched for? Is the title of their listing short or is it so long that Google has truncated it? You'll probably notice that their brand name is included in the title as well - is it shown at the start or end of the title?

Now look at the description underneath the title of their listing. How many times do the keywords show up in the description? Does it read like normal writing, or is it broken up with ellipsis? Broken up descriptions tends to mean that Google has chosen to ignore the description they've provided, and instead taken text from the website itself.

Notice what sort of titles and descriptions you can see on the page. The Google results page contains a huge amount of information relevant to our mission so it's worth spending some more time noticing which descriptions and titles stand out or make you want to click on the link. We can borrow from these enticing titles and descriptions later on.

Once you've made a mental note of your main target's description and titles in the results page, it's time to click on the link to their site.

Notice which page opens when you click on the link – is it the homepage: e.g.

www.petesmechanics.com or is it a different page, e.g. www.petesmechanics.com/mots-in-croydon?

On the best SEO'd sites, you'll notice that the address of the page that opens contains the keywords you searched for. In the example above, you'll see that the page petesmechanics.com/mots-in-croydon contains the words "MOTs" "In" and "Croydon". This is good practice and we'll be looking at how to do this later on.

It also usually means that this page has been targeted specifically at the keywords "MOTs in Croydon".

Next we're going to have a look to see how many times the phrase you initially searched for shows up on your competitor's webpage.

Press CTRL+F if you're on a PC or cmd+F if you're on a Mac, and type in the phrase you searched for.

You'll see how many times the keywords have been used on the page. This number might be anything from 0 on very poorly SEO'd sites to 30+ on over-SEO'd sites. It will usually be somewhere in the middle.

Next, find how many times the individual words in the phrase appear, and also any variations, for example "roofer", "roofing", "roof". Google understands that they refer to the same thing and it's a good idea to include keyword variations on your page. Have your competitors used variations of the keywords in their text?

The next thing we are going to do is look under the hood of your competitor's site to see the optimisation they've used in the page's code, as sometimes they will have left telltale signs of their strategy that we can 'borrow'...

Right click on the side of the page, away from the text and picture content, and click View Source (also sometimes called View Page Source or something similar).

The page's source code will open in a new window. We are looking for a couple of sections in particular:

The first is a line that begins: `<meta name="keywords`...

If this line exists, then the website owner has at least attempted to optimise their website to show up on Google. If you look further along in the line, you'll see the list of keywords they have chosen to target with their website.

Whilst you shouldn't assume that they have got the 'right' list, it can be really helpful to see which keywords they've chosen and there might be some that you haven't thought of. The point of all this research is just to absorb what your competitors are doing before we decide how and where to attack.

The next section we're going to look at starts `<title>`. What follows this `<title>` tag is the title of the page that showed up in the Google search. It's worth looking through this title to see how many times they have used the keyword you searched for, and any variations. If this title doesn't contain the keyword or phrase (perhaps just their brand name), it's good news because it's a strong indication that their site is not properly optimised. This page title is one of the most important factors on the entire website to determine where it ranks, and for which phrases, so if they've got their brand name on its own there, that's a total waste of an area that should be used for targeting keywords.

Now find the `<meta name="description"` section. If you can't find it, again that can mean that the site is under-optimised and this is great news.
But for most websites that have been even slightly optimised, the `<meta name="description"` section will contain a brief description of the webpage. This description is the suggested descriptive text for search engines to use in the search results, although Google will choose to display text from the page itself if it believes that it's more relevant to the search and content of the page.

This Meta description can give us some valuable insight into the SEO techniques of your competitors, because people tend to fill it with their target keywords in a summary of what they think their searchers are looking for.

We'll be looking at Meta Descriptions later on, but for now another indication to the level of optimisation of the site is the length of the Meta Descriptions on your competitors' sites. Google tends to truncate at around 160 characters, so very long or short Meta Descriptions tend to be a symptom of an improperly optimised site.

Close the source code, and head back to the website.

A really important point: It's generally good practice to have a separate page targeting each of your main keywords. This page will contain the keyword in the page title and the URL. The keyword should be found plenty of times in the text content, plus variations and modifiers. (Variations are obviously different forms of the same word: roofer, roofing, roof. Modifiers are what we call 'add on' words – so for example for the keyword: plumber, one modifier might be 'emergency' as in 'emergency plumber'.)

Try to notice if your competitors have plenty of different pages all focussed on different keywords, so spend some time clicking through their navigation to see how many pages they have that appear to target specific keywords. They might not be linked to from the main navigation section and you might have to dig a little deeper to find them. A good way to make sure that you're not missing any pages is to look through their sitemap. To do this, just Google their website address plus the word sitemap (e.g. "exposureninja.com sitemap") and click on the result that ends /sitemap.xml. This will give you a comprehensive list of the pages on their site, so you can see any pages not listed in their main navigation.

You'll sometimes notice that these keyword-targeted pages are linked to from a section of links in or near the website's footer. The reason people do this is to avoid cluttering the layout of their website with links to dozens of pages, whilst still linking to them from every page. So they effectively 'sweep them under the carpet' and bury them right at the bottom out of sight.

This technique is increasingly seen as just the wrong side of being spammy, and while it's OK to have pages targeting different phrases, you need to make sure that the linked pages are genuinely high quality and useful to visitors. And avoid the spammy-looking footer links!

Once you are satisfied that you have mentally logged all the different pages on your competitor's site, noticed which keywords they are shooting for and seen how many times they're using the keywords on their pages, you can move on to your next competitor.

This might seem like a lot of work, but trust me – this is a major shortcut to years of trial and error!

Backlinks

Remember that Google likes sites that have a lot of links pointing at them because this indicates that they're popular or considered authoritative.

The next step in your SEO detective work is to analyse the number and quality of backlinks yours and your competitors' sites have.

Head over to http://moz.com/researchtools/ose and put in your website's address. The tool will give you an indication of how many backlinks your site has, and the total number of sites linking to you. (If you're not seeing many links you can also check out http://backlinkwatch.com)

At the top of the Open Site Explorer page you'll see a number of statistics:
- Domain authority. This is an estimate of the site's PageRank, so is an indication of authority. The more high quality inbound links a site has, the higher the domain authority will be.
- Page authority. This is an estimate of the specific page's PageRank (rather than the website in its entirety).
- The Established links section shows how many individual sites (Root domains) and total links point at the website.

By putting in your top competitors' sites in for comparison, you can begin to identify possible reasons why they might be outranking you. If you're being outranked, you'll usually find that your competitors have more links and higher Domain and Page Authority.

Opensite Explorer will show you a selection of the inbound links, whereas Backlink Watch will show you the page and anchor text used in each link.

Anchor Text

Anchor text is the text used in a link. When you're surfing on the net, you might see an underlined word in blue, something like <u>click here</u>.

Obviously clicking on that link won't take you to a website called 'click here', those words are what we call the anchor text.

So why is anchor text important from an SEO standpoint?

The reason we love anchor text is because it can identify what the webpage on the other end of the link is about. For example, in the 'click here' example, Google would see the words 'click here' and associate the linked page with that phrase.

Hopefully then you can also see that using 'click here' as anchor text is not the best idea in the world.

A far better idea would to use your keywords as anchor text, for example <u>vintage furniture</u> for a site that sells vintage furniture. You can see the anchor text your competitors are using by choosing the *Anchor Text* tab in Open Site Explorer. If you notice that they always have the same backlink text, take note because this is likely the phrase they have singled out above all others to rank highly for.

It might seem like a good idea to create lots of links using your main keyword as the anchor text, but this is where you have to start being careful. This strategy was used to death by low quality SEO companies in the past to the extent where Google's Penguin update actually started *penalising* sites for using too much 'exact match anchor text', where the anchor text *exactly matches* the target keyword. It's natural for websites to get a lot of links with their company name and website address as anchor text, so this is what Google expects to see in a natural-looking link profile. If 80% of the inbound links say <u>vintage furniture</u>, that starts to look a bit suspect.

When building links then, it's a good idea to use descriptive anchor text as long as you're being natural. Mix it up a bit and use different keywords.

On with the Competitor Analysis...

By now you should have a list of the keywords you plan to target and a list of your top competitors for those keywords.

You will have studied their websites and noticed the keywords they are targeting, and how aggressively they are targeting them by making a mental note of the frequency of those keywords on the page, in links and in the Meta description and `<title>` tags, as well as the Meta keywords section.
Phew!

Reader Offer: Free SEO and Website audit

Remember that you can claim your completely free SEO and website audit from Exposure Ninja, the Web and SEO company I run, by heading over to www.exposureninja.com/audit

You'll receive a personalised prescription with suggestions for boosting your ranking and conversion as well as some tips for general SEO best practice.

Before we leave your competitors' sites, we're just going to take a quick look at the structure of their websites. By structure, we mean how the pages are ordered.

Most well designed websites have pages at different 'levels'. For example top-level pages might be called Home, Contact, Services, Products etc. These pages have pages underneath them (second-level pages) that go into more detail. For example Services might break into 'Ladies' and 'Gents' on a hair salon website. These second-level pages might then break into yet more pages covering each of the individual services on offer, for example:

Services (top-level page) -> Ladies (second-level page) -> Wedding Hair (third-level page)

As well as giving your website visitors a simple and intuitive way to navigate your website, having an organized structure means that you can optimize each of your third-level pages to make them laser targeted. For example, the page 'Wedding Hair' can be optimized fully for the phrase *Wedding Hair*, without having to try and work in other target keywords like 'hair colouring' and 'full head spiral perm' (I had to look that one up). Pages so specifically targeted stand a really good chance of showing up on Google.

It also means your website visitors don't have to trawl through a ton of information about something they might have no interest in (wedding hair) just to find the content they thought they were clicking through to (spiral perms), increasing conversion rate.

Your Website

This is a good opportunity to talk about your website, and specifically how much control you have over it. One of the key barriers to SEO success for many businesses is an out-of-date website that is uneconomical to make any changes to. Some are held prisoner by unresponsive or unreliable freelance web designers who wield ultimate say over what happens to the site, whereas others control the site themselves but have no idea how to make the necessary changes to get their site ranking.

For some very small businesses, software like Wordpress makes building your own website a genuine possibility, although with many of the more advanced themes now requiring professional-level coding skill, anyone with the budget to use a professional developer generally sees a far higher return on that investment than does the DIY-er.

What many businesses fail to realise is that holding on to an out-of-date and poorly optimised website is costing them far more in lost business than getting a professionally built website would.

To rank well on Google and convert the resulting traffic profitably, you need a site that represents your business in a way that you're truly proud of and converts visitors to buyers, at the same time as allowing you to make the SEO changes in this book. If you don't have this, it should be your top marketing priority.

What many businesses don't realise is that even with a well SEO'd site, the layout and design of the site itself can hold back ranking. Google takes into consideration how visitors respond to a website, if there's a high bounce rate, if the site is or isn't mobile-friendly etc. and this all has an effect on ranking. If your website hasn't been updated in the last 2 years, this is typically one of those 'low hanging fruit' areas.

Niche keywords

If you are competing in a very competitive niche, you might be up against some serious players with a huge amount of online clout, thousands of quality backlinks, subscribers, email lists, busy social media channels and all the rest.

An example might be a local bank fighting it out with the big multinationals, a local bookstore or London plumber fighting against a vast array of competitors with more established online presences.

If this is the case, then it might not make sense to fight for the most common keywords. If typing in 'plumber' brings up a page of extremely well optimised plumbers and powerful national directory sites, it's going to be a hard-fought battle to come out on top. That's not to say you *can't* or *won't* come out on top, but you'll expend vast amounts of energy competing in a competitive game when there might be a more productive use of that time and energy.

Likewise, if you're pushed for time and just want an immediate spike in your results you might also try the strategy I'm about to share.

In virtually all markets, as well as the main keywords, there are more niched keywords. These are searches being performed by fewer people than the more general keywords, but they are more specialised and qualified searchers. Depending on the niche, they can even be *more valuable* customers or be more likely to buy as a result of visiting your site.

Let's look at some examples:

A hair salon fighting a lot of local competition might want to specialize in wedding hair or colouring, and advertise themselves online as the local specialist in this area. This gives them a smaller pool of local competition and allows them to get to the top of Google faster. So rather than targeting the keyword "hair salon" they might choose to target "wedding hair <area>" instead. They'll find it much easier to rank for this 'longer tail' keyword, and will generally find it a more efficient use of their time. It's better to be page one for a second level keyword than page 10 for a superstar keyword!

Some people mistakenly think that targeting these niche keywords means that they are surrendering or admitting defeat by choosing to eat from a smaller pie. What they don't realise is that by targeting the more niche keywords, they might actually get *more* business as a result. Not only are there fewer competitors chasing each customer, but also the customers like to feel they are buying from a specialist and therefore the implication is that the product or service will be of greater quality. They will be able to charge higher prices and will find people attaching higher perceived value to dealing with 'the specialist'. So choosing to niche in the face of heavy competition from established players can not only make good SEO sense but good business sense.

It's likely that many of the keywords you've written down will be niche keywords to some extent, and having sized up your competitors you will now be able to decide whether you fancy competing for the broad keywords or want to develop more towards the niche keywords at least to begin with.

For the more aggressive, yes, you *can* do both!

Black Hat (Secret, Underground, Illegal) Strategies vs. White Hat

(Clean, Legal) Strategies and when to use each one

As well as legitimate ways to make your website show up higher in the rankings (like the ones in this book), there are a number of 'other' strategies which some less scrupulous Search Engine Optimisers use to get websites up the rankings.
The advantage of any 'black hat' or improper, devious or spammy techniques is that they can work. Very well. For a time, at least.

The disadvantage is that Google doesn't like black hat, and is constantly working to identify and punish websites that use black hat strategies. As time goes on, they get better and better at spotting them, and along with each Google update comes a more aggressive stance against those who try to manipulate search rankings by using spam. Many of the SEOs complaining about Google Penguin penalties are guilty of being lazy or using Black Hat techniques rather than putting the time and effort into using good White Hat human-focussed promotion.

While it can be tempting to peer over to the dark side and think about submitting your website to link farms (websites which can give a lot of low quality backlinks by linking to other websites which link back to them), automated spamming software and other ways to get lots and lots of backlinks with no effort, just bear in mind that, if it hasn't already, Google will catch up with you at some point.

And when that point comes, they might choose to punish you by giving a ranking penalty or removing you from their listings (deindexing) completely. It is entirely up to them and you would have no say in the matter. They have a history of doing it, and they are unafraid to flex their muscles.

Every day we get desperate emails from website owners who have bought low quality links in the past and their sites have disappeared from the Google results page they relied upon to bring them new customers. Their business has suffered and they are desperate, begging for help.

One of the most striking cases I've experienced was getting an early morning call from the owner of a dental practice. She had been referred to me as Google penalties had all but destroyed her business. Calling from a nearby car park, she tearily explained that she couldn't face going into the practice that was struggling to attract new bookings thanks to the loss of all Google ranking. Staff had been laid off and she feared having to lay off more. In her case there was a happy ending, as successful link disavowal led to a massive recovery of all lost rankings, and on-going SEO is helping to increase their visibility further. But not everyone is so lucky.

It's quite sad to see, so please don't be tempted. By the way, if this sounds a little *too* familiar, then keep reading...

As time goes on, the black hat techniques evolve. Currently, it's very easy to buy large numbers of links very cheaply from websites like Fiverr. Some of these links are really low quality link farms, but others appear to offer good value legitimate opportunities to get links that are currently not attracting penalties (they are considered 'Penguin Safe'):

- Manual submissions to social bookmarking websites
- Social media links including:
    - Retweets
    - Posts
    - Pinterest Pins

The danger of using these types of shortcuts is that it's a case of *when* rather than *if* Google catches up with them and they lose their effectiveness (or even become harmful to ranking). You can rest assured that some of the smartest minds on the planet are processing huge amounts of data *right now,* with the aim of identifying tell tale signs of social media spamming behaviour and fake accounts. By dipping your toe into this water you risk being punished later on.

Hidden text and cloaking are two popular 'on page' techniques traditionally used by black hat SEOs. They are seen less frequently however, as the sites that use them disappear from search results. Nevertheless, they are useful techniques to understand so you can spot them whilst surfing.

Because Google and other search engines look at the text on a website's pages in order to work out what the site is all about, some people will add a huge amount of keyword-rich text to the page in order to give the search engine more 'meat' to chew on. The thinking is that with all that great content, the search engine will reward the website by placing it high in the rankings.

The problem is that a page with this amount of text on can be very off-putting for visitors to the site. So black hat SEOs will hide this text on the page. They might give it the same colour as the background so it's invisible to people reading the site, or they might position it off screen.

The end result is that they can make the page look how they want, whilst also making something that Google sees as content rich.

Another benefit for hiding the content was that it could be written purely for the benefit of search engines, stuffed so full of keywords that it was virtually unreadable.

However, Google wised up to this sort of keyword spam and now understands text readability, using it as a ranking factor, penalising unnaturally keyword stuffed copy. So a much better approach (for SEO and visitors) is to write good keyword-rich text that your website visitors actually want to read and will find interesting & useful. That way they will stay on your page, perhaps link or share the content, and be more likely to convert.

Another black hat strategy employed by SEOs is 'cloaking' pages; that is present a different page depending on whether a human or search engine is looking at the site. With cloaking, black hat SEOs can make the page rank highly in Google and then send you to whatever page they want. It might be a similar page or it might be a totally unrelated page. Again, this is similar to the hidden text method in that it means the SEO can show Google a page that is extremely content-rich but send the user to a page that is not burdened with large amounts of text. This was a relatively common thing for owners of Flash websites to do but as the world has moved *away* from flash and towards text-based websites, cloaking for legitimate means has all but disappeared. It's now extremely rare that you'll see a website using cloaking appear in the Google results.

White Hat SEO

So what about white hat techniques? Most SEO companies combine white and grey hat techniques to satisfy their clients' impatience for fast results. The downside of grey hat techniques is that today's grey hat becomes tomorrow's black hat, and strategies that once seemed just a little devious end up attracting Google's wrath.

For long-term focussed businesses, there's really no justification to stray over to black hat strategies. Sticking to white hat, Google-approved strategies gives you the peace of mind and restful sleep around the time of Google updates that the black hatters don't get. High profile penalties for sites like Interflora, Halifax and Expedia show that size is no protection from immunity. If you spam, you usually *do* get caught eventually.

The strategies we'll be talking about in the remainder of this book all fall into the category of what is currently considered 'white hat'.

Your Website

Your website is absolutely central to getting better visibility on Google. The best links in the world can't compensate for an awful website, and a good quality, well-optimised, Google readable site can take you a good part of the way to market domination. A lot of businesses need to take a step back and ask "does this look like the sort of website that would be at the top of Google?" If the honest answer is no, then that's the first thing to work on.

However good a website is, it needs to be search engine optimised if it's to rank well. SEO work done to a website itself is known as Onsite SEO. Onsite SEO can be summarised as *organising the information on your website in a way that gives Google what it needs to rank it highly.*

We're going to look at a number of different strategies to make your website easily readable by Google, demonstrate its relevance and make sure that all your relevant pages are indexed and showing up in search results.

But first, some words about different website platforms:

I and many other people who like getting to the top of Google use Wordpress websites. Wordpress is an awesome (and free!) platform which makes it dead easy to maintain your website. If you're starting your website building activities from scratch, 9 times out of 10 my advice would be to USE WORDPRESS! As well as being easy to use, Google really likes Wordpress and finds Wordpress sites very easy to read. Pretty much the only time that we'd recommend a non-Wordpress website is for large E-commerce stores or custom platforms.

If your site is built on another platform, fear not. A well built and optimised website will rank well on Google however it's coded.

The exception is if your website is heavily flash-based. If your site has lots of fancy animation and when you click on different pages the link in the top bar doesn't change, it might be time to consider leaving it behind. Many clients don't like hearing that their old Wix flash websites are never going to get to the top of Google but the truth is that Google simply CAN'T read flash. Fewer and fewer people are building with flash and it is becoming obsolete because of the rise of popularity of HTML5, which does a lot of the same stuff and *is* Google-readable.

If you don't mind about Google placement and are ok with people on iPhones and iPads not being able to use your website, then Flash is fine. But its days are numbered and I strongly recommend looking at alternatives.

Since publishing this book, we receive a lot of emails from folks who have heard about the joys of Wordpress and other Content Management

Systems (CMS), and are considering having their website rebuilt using one. With SEO relying so heavily on keeping content fresh and updating the site frequently, we're big fans of websites that allow owners to have control.

There are 3 reasons we recommend using a Content Management System like Wordpress for your website:

1. You will have greater control over the content on the site and will be able to update it more frequently (for example by writing a blog), which has huge benefits for SEO.
2. A lot of the on-page SEO we'll be covering in this book is much easier and quicker if you are using a CMS.
3. If you want to change the look and feel or layout of your website later on, you can do this relatively simply and you won't have lost all your content or on-page SEO, future-proofing it.

If you'd like to know more about moving your site over to Wordpress, just Google "exposure ninja moving over to Wordpress" to find our blog post guide.

Domains & URLs

Your address or 'URL' can have a significant impact on your website's success, both from ranking and branding perspectives.

Addressing the ranking side of things first, before

Google's 2012 EMD update it was ridiculously easy to rank websites using 'Exact Match Domains' - website addresses that *exactly matched* what searchers were looking for. If you wanted to get to the top of Google for "flower shop Nottingham" for example, you could just set up www.flowershopnottingham.com and wait for the money to roll in. We could rank sites within a day or two based *purely* on the domain in some cases, which meant we didn't have to worry about troublesome things like content and links. While it's true that the power of the EMD is not as significant as it once was, we're still seeing domains with keywords have an edge over their competitors that don't.

But even without the EMD benefit, it can often make sense to use a more descriptive domain for your site. If a fictional accounting firm E Smith & Son, based in Bury has the choice between www.accountantsbury.com and www.esmithandson.com, the more memorable and instantly descriptive domain name would be the first. If a Google searcher types "accountants Bury", they're going to see a website address which exactly matches what they're looking for, and the site is clearly relevant.

Key EMD Myths

Many businesses have at some point bought up large numbers of EMDs related to their industry. One of their first questions is "*is there any benefit to pointing all of these domains at our main website?*" The answer is no. The only way that these EMDs would be of use is if you are to build up separate, fully functional websites for each of them with unique targeted content giving the site a high relevance for that phrase. Simply redirecting them to your main site gives no SEO benefit because Google is just not that gameable!

The second myth is that using an EMD actually *harms* your ranking. People talk of the EMD update as a penalty, in the same way that other Google updates have penalised sites. In reality the EMD update *removed some of the advantage* rather than installing a *disadvantage*. The perception of a 'penalty' exists because sites that once enjoyed a significant benefit saw this was removed, and they might have noticed a subsequent ranking drop.

Differences between TLDs

A common question is about the difference between different Top Level Domains (TLDs), for example .com, .co.uk, .org and .ninja.

As a rule, don't copy our Marketing Training Platform (www.marketingu.ninja) and instead use a common TLD. '.com' or country-specific is best, and .biz, .name and .info are typically considered indicators of a low quality site. For MarketingU, .ninja was just too appropriate to ignore!

Competition for .com and country-specific domains is far higher than for the unusual TLDs.

That means that those setting up low quality spam sites tend to find it easier to get an available .biz domain than the .com version. Hence these domains have been used (and ruined) by a high proportion of low quality spam websites to the extent where seeing one of these domains in the wild raises red flags for search engines.

Hyphens and Separators

As a rule, avoid use of hyphens in your domain as this too is seen as a spam indicator. Spammy sites often use hyphens in order to fit their target keywords in the URL once the most popular .com domains were taken, so it tends to be considered a spam trigger.

Domain Length

While we haven't seen any conclusive proof or a relationship between domain length and SEO friendliness, choosing a domain less than 14-16 characters makes a lot of sense. Firstly it's easier to remember and type correctly, resulting in less lost traffic as a result of misspellings. Secondly, long domains tend to cause problems in Adwords ads, as they can be too long to fit in the Display URL section of an Ad.

Domain Age

The age of your domain *can* have a significant effect on your ranking for a couple of reasons:

Firstly an older domain signals to Google that the site has been established longer, so is therefore more likely to be a reputable business and less likely to use short-term spammy tactics.

Secondly, sites tend to pick up links as they age, which can give aged domains more authority than a brand-new domain.

One myth is that the length of domain registration has an effect on ranking. The reasoning is that if you register your domain for a long time, you must plan to keep the site for a long time, and therefore be less likely to be a 'churn and burn' spammer!

While this makes logical sense, Google's spam fighting super ninja Matt Cutts has publicly declared that this doesn't have an effect on ranking. Shame!

Mobile Friendliness

In 2014, mobile search traffic across all our clients' sites increased *fifty per cent*. FIFTY per cent! This is a HUGE trend and one that Google looks very closely at. Unfortunately, much of the Internet is yet to catch up with the increase in mobile Internet usage and many websites are pretty horrible on mobile phones and tablets.

Making sure that your website is mobile friendly is a key factor in getting it ranking prominently these days. Sites that aren't mobile friendly frustrate users who have to pinch and zoom to see content, click tiny buttons with fat fingers and scroll vertically. This frustration shows in user behaviour, and you can see it in Google Analytics: typically a site will have a bounce rate of approximately 45% (meaning that 45% of visitors click away before visiting a second page). But if you look at a non-mobile friendly site, the bounce rate on mobile will typically be from 65-80%.

You might be tempted to sweep this under the carpet, but keep in mind that Google sees these statistics. Any site with a 65% bounce rate is extremely unlikely to rank well, and Google will be very reluctant to show the site to searchers if it's getting such a significant down vote. Usage statistics are an important ranking metric so pleasing users on any device is a very good idea.

There are two main ways to make your site mobile friendly. The first is to build in 'responsive' behaviour. This means that the site will reorganise itself to fit on smaller screens, positioning its elements in a vertical line for easy scrolling. The benefit of this method is that because everyone sees the same website (it's just reorganised per device) you have only to maintain the one site. The downside is that with a complicated site there can be a lot of technical coding work required to make the site responsive.

The alternative method to make a site mobile-friendly is through a separate mobile website. When a user visits your site, if their screen is below a certain size they'll see the mobile version which has been designed specifically to work on mobile. You'll have two separate websites to maintain, but on the plus side the mobile site can be built separately without any disruption to the main website.

The good news about mobile friendliness is that any website designer worth their salt will build it in as standard with any new site, and if you're using Wordpress many themes are now responsive as standard. It's such an important thing that if your site is not already mobile friendly, sorting this should be one of your top priorities.

Multiple Websites

Lots of people ask about the feasibility of building multiple websites to target different locations, and this used to be our standard advice when a content-light site with an exact match domain name was all that was required to rank well. However, it's no longer so clear-cut and in most cases, promoting one single site across multiple locations can make a lot of sense.

For example a courier company with three city bases might have set up separate sites targeting each local office, using site addresses like www.courierliverpool.co.uk, www.couriermanchester.co.uk. All of the content on each of these websites could be locally targeted, with branding kept consistent across all the sites. Nowadays though it makes more sense to create one awesome website with different pages targeting each of the local offices. That way links boosting the authority of the main site will benefit all of the individual locations, rather than having to raise the authority of a number of sites.

Therefore the most common approach nowadays is to simply create new pages on the business's existing site that are targeted at each of their local services. As well as saving time and effort, this approach has another couple of benefits:
1. The new pages are part of a well-established site, taking some benefit from existing PageRank, domain age and authority whilst making the existing site more authoritative.
2. Being part of a larger website gives these pages more credibility, increasing conversion rate and sales.
3. Link building and offsite promotion can be directed at just one domain.

One case where we have opted to combine a number of microsites is for a large global e-commerce store with 8 separate country-level microsites. The headache they had was optimising and promoting 8 different websites and rewriting content for 750 products to avoid duplicate content. They also wanted to make each site multilingual, so would need to get each site's content translated separately. That's 750 products, written up 8 different times, with each being translated in 4 languages. Nightmare.

In this situation, we opted to amalgamate the local sites into one global site. This site automatically detects the country each visitor is in and shows them the local prices for the products, the local contact information and uses their native language (although this can be switched). Each of the existing country specific domains was directed at the new site making the visitor transition seamless, the team now has the far simpler task of keeping one site updated, and the link building work doesn't need to be spread across 8 different sites.

Multiple 'microsites' can still be a good option for businesses that have distinct customer groups or entirely separate products that don't share an audience though.

One example is a dental client we have in Birmingham that also owns a cosmetic enhancement clinic. We opted to keep the two websites completely separate as the dental practice was mainly targeted at families whilst the beauty clinic has a completely different target audience. In order to laser (no pun intended) target each site to their respective audience, the imagery, language and target keywords needed to be completely separate, and the most effective way to do this was through distinct sites.

Another of our clients offered stress management, anxiety treatment and peak performance coaching. To promote each of these distinct services, we set up smaller 'feeder' or 'satellite' sites targeting one specific category (for example stress management) which then allows us to optimise not just the page, but the entire site (and domain) for this key phrase and related key phrases (like 'stress symptoms', 'treatments for stress' etc.).

Each of these satellite sites is written individually, linked to a separate Google+ profile, submitted and indexed separately – as if they were completely separate businesses. As a result, the client has a number of top position results for each of the different services he offers, in addition to his main website which also now ranks very highly.

The obvious downside of this approach is that it involves a lot more work. Text needs to be completely rewritten for each of the sites to avoid duplicate content issues (covered later on), and the business has the job of maintaining and building links to two sites.

So the decision to microsite or not to microsite really depends on the specific case. If it's possible to logically combine everything onto one site, that's the easiest and most sensible way to do it. However if the customer groups are distinct or the messaging needs to be different, niche microsites make a lot of sense.

We've already had a brief look at website structure in the last section where you examined the structure of your competitors' websites, so now it's time to audit your own website's structure and make sure it is fully optimized. What follows is the internal Exposure Ninja structure guidelines that we use when we build sites for clients.

With a pen and paper (we tend to favour going old school for this exercise) draw boxes across the top of the page for each of your website's top-level pages. By top-level pages, we mean the main pages visible on your menu.

As an example, an e-commerce site selling Ninja Clothing might have the following top-level pages:
- Homepage
- Clothing
- Accessories
- The Ninja Club
- Delivery & Returns
- About Us

These are all pages that general visitors to the Ninja Clothing Store site would be interested in. If a shopper wanted to browse for Ninja Weapons, they'd go to *Accessories* and a drop down would appear which included the *Ninja Weapons* category. There'd be no need to have a *Ninja Weapons* tab on the main menu, because including every category would extend the menu beyond what is practical, confusing visitors.

An example of an over-cluttered e-commerce menu

Think of it like a shop window: you don't want to put *every single* product you sell in the shop window *but you want people who are looking for something in particular to know where they can find it*.

Next we're going to add our second level pages, drawn below our top-level pages and linked with a line. Second-level pages are more specific and start to drill down into the products or services that you offer.

In e-commerce, second level pages are usually Category pages listing all the products of a particular type; engagement rings or long sleeved t-shirts, for example.

In the ninja clothing store, there are a few different categories of clothing:
• Full Ninja suits
• Jackets
• Balaclavas
• Tabi Boots

From our top-level Accessories page comes four second-level pages:
• Punching bags

- Weapons
- Headbands
- Bags

Next, we're going to add the third-level pages. These pages drill down into another level of detail. Not every website needs third level pages, but if you sell a wider variety of products or services, adding them can help your customers (and search engines) quickly get to the right category.

For our Ninja Clothing store, I decide that punching bags is a second level page that doesn't need another level of detail. However, after talking to my customers, I discover that they tend to be much more likely to search for "Ninja star" or "ninja staff" than the more general phrase "ninja weapons". So I decide to add a second level of detail underneath the Weapons page by adding third level pages:
- Shuriken
- Ninja Stars
- Swords
- Nunchucks
...and so on.

At this stage we're still not fleshing out the content for the pages but deciding the overall structure of the site.

For local businesses that serve a number of different areas, it's a good idea to include pages targeting each local area. Searchers tend to add locations to local searches (for example "builders in Brixton" or "Chinese restaurants CM2"), and by having locally targeted pages you can begin to pick up some organic search results in addition to map results.

Let's look at an example: Harry's Home Extensions builds home extensions for people in and around Southampton, UK. Because Southampton is quite a big city, residents looking for a builder to do their extension might be unlikely to search "home extensions Southampton". Some will, no doubt, but many more will use their local area as the location modifier instead. Some of the areas within Southampton that Harry finds himself doing a lot of work in are Whiteley, Hedge End and Warsash, so he decides to make a separate page for each of these areas.

He calls these pages "Home Extensions Whiteley", "Home Extensions Hedge End" and "Home Extensions Warsash". On these pages he describes some of the projects that his company has carried out, making sure to include local information (such as the roads that the properties were on). He also lists some of the postcodes in the area and writes a unique overview of the service his company offers and why homeowners choose them to build their home extensions. By the time the site is finished, there are individual area-targeted pages with 400+ words of locally targeted content, pictures from past jobs and some testimonials from people local to the area.

For a business like Home Extensions, optimising these pages and making sure they get indexed will likely be enough to have them rank top or very highly for their main target phrases. Not only this, but visitors landing on these pages have a higher chance of converting because the content is *so* relevant to them.

So whether you're an e-commerce site or not, these first, second and third level pages mean that your audience can find really useful information collected in one place. From an SEO point of view it means that you've got an entire page on your site targeted to a particular search, which gives you a significant boost in the competition to have the most relevant website and get top ranking.

Yes, this means building quite a few pages for your website. Rejoice in the effort this takes, because this is the effort that will set you apart from your competitors who don't invest in doing what it takes to get to the top of Google.

URL Structure

If your website uses ugly, codey URLs for your pages, neither Google nor users can tell the contents of a page just by looking at the link.

What do I mean by ugly codey links? Links that look like this:
https://ninjaclothingstore.com/?=314

It's the ?=314 bit at the end that is the ugly bit. Much better is the following:

https://ninjaclothingstore.com/accessories/weapons/shuriken

Any human who sees this link can figure out that this page contains information about ninja weapons, in particular shuriken. Google can read this too, and it acts as a vote of confidence for the site to show for "Ninja Shuriken" searches.

How your page URLs appear typically depends how your website is built. For some people, there's no (simple) way to change the format of their URLs. If you have a Wordpress site, it is incredibly easy to change this structure however. Simply go into your dashboard, click Settings, choose Permalinks and then the /postname/ option and click save. You are now using what are called 'pretty' permalinks.
It is beyond the scope of this book to go into detail about every possible website platform and how to change link structure but it is worth spending some time making sure that your permalinks are nice and easy to read for humans and robots alike.

It's also worth noting that being logical with your URLs is enough. There's no need to stuff every possible keyword into your URLs, and in fact Google tries to penalise this sort of 'keyword stuffing'. Make it logical and obvious and you will be fine.

Because websites can get pretty complicated when they contain lots of pages, it's a good idea to build a sitemap. This is a map of the website's page structure that we submit Google, ensuring that its spiders are *aware* of every page on your site.

Without going into the details of creating your sitemap (if you're on Wordpress use the Google XML Sitemap Plugin), there are usually two types:
1. XML
2. HTML

XML sitemaps are designed purely for Google. They contain code that tells Google how often it should recrawl the page, and the relative significance of every page. Because it's created for Google, it tends to be unformatted and look quite 'code-y'.

HTML sitemaps on the other hand *are* intended for human consumption. They are usually formatted in the same style as the rest of the site's pages, and because they're coded in HTML they use a clearer layout that also indicates the page hierarchy.

Usually an HTML sitemap is unnecessary unless the navigation of the website is so poor that visitors have to resort to scanning through a list of the site's pages to find the information they need. If you have an HTML sitemap on your site and you notice from your Google Analytics data that it's being used with any significant frequency, take this as a warning sign and rebuild your navigation!

Writing for your website

The content of your website is one of the very most important components and contributors to your online success. Despite this, it's often treated as an afterthought in the website development process and produced without the consideration it really deserves.

Let's look at how to write awesome website content and start fleshing out all those pages you've planned for your site.

The key when writing the text for your web pages is to first and foremost make it human friendly. There's no point being top of Google if your website visitors are put off by the words on your page sounding spammy because you've stuffed them so full of keywords. Remember also that Google uses usage statistics to influence ranking, so if visitors aren't staying on your pages to read your text, this will affect your long-term ranking. Finally, Google uses readability algorithms as an onsite signal for the quality of a website's content, so keyword stuffing will no longer even bring a benefit.

Having said that, it's obviously important to keep an SEO perspective on everything you write.

Using your keywords correctly in text *is* important, as is making sure that the layout complies with web best practices.

The first step when you sit down to write for a particular page is to keep in mind the specific keyword or phrase that this page is designed to represent. For our Ninja Clothing Store, on the Clothing -> Balaclavas page, we're going to write with the phrase "Ninja Balaclava" in mind as our *primary keyword*.

A good starting point is to use your main keyword in the title at the top of the page. If you are writing in HTML, put your keyword in <h1> tags at the top. If you're not getting all code-y, then make your title Heading 1 in the editor. This is a clear demonstration to Google that this phrase is particularly important to the page. As a rule, you'll only use one H1 heading on that page, so the fact that it uses the phrase Ninja Balaclavas is a sign to Google that you're confident that the topic of the page is this phrase.

If you can get away without sounding too spammy, you can then use a variation of your keyword or phrase in an <h2> or Heading 2 underneath this main title.

For example:
<h1>Ninja Balaclavas</h1>
<h2>Buy Ninja headgear from the UK's Ninja Balaclava Specialists</h2>

You'll see we've used the word Ninja three times (frequently, but not overused), Balaclava twice, and the word Headgear. Use of "buy" tells Google and visitors this is a commercial site suitable for commercial searches.

This type of heading and subheading really gets you off to a great start, and it's a formula that you should use for every page.

If you are a local business, remember to include plenty of mentions of your location in all your website's pages. If you serve a number of different locations, mention of them briefly on product or category pages, then link through to the specific targeted area pages we discussed above to enhance the local association.

One of the most common SEO questions is *how much do I need to write for each page?*

The main problem we face when optimising websites is that long boring pages of text turn off users, increase bounce rate and ultimately hurt conversion. On the other hand, search engines need to see enough content on a page to understand its meaning and recognise its authority. The guideline has always been 350-400 words per page, but sometimes people struggle to come up with enough good quality content to get anywhere near this target.

One strategy is to first write the headings you'll use down the page. You can then lean on these headings to come up with enough content. Think that it might be hard to write 400 words about Ninja Balaclavas? Without breaking up the text in different sections, it probably would be. But using headlines you'll see that each section only needs around 80 words to hit that target:

- Types of Ninja Balaclava
- History of the Balaclava
- Ninja Balaclava FAQs
- How to Choose Your Perfect Balaclava
- Our Balaclava Warranty

When we're planning a website for a client, a common request is that we avoid the use of 'too much text' because it spoils the design. This is a fair point as long lines of unbroken copy are extremely tiring to read, and frankly, who can be bothered? The problem is that the text is extremely important; Google needs it, and actually in most cases, it's still the primary method of communicating with the *visitors* on your website. No text, no message. And no message, no sale.

The solution is in how the text is presented. Compare the layout of a pick-me-up magazine to a technical journal, and you'll see how text can be presented in a fun and engaging way to catch readers. Using short paragraphs, narrow columns, sub headlines, pictures (with captions, the second most read part of the page after headlines) and expandable accordion sections can make your pages playful and interesting rather than dull and text-y.

Repeat this process for each and every page. Like anything worthwhile it does take some effort, but rejoice at this – will your competitors put this effort in?

One of the neatest tricks to Google domination is securing multiple listings on the results page. In one case we were able to get a site showing up in top position, and a further five times in the next 6 results on page one. In total, this business had six of the top 7 results. This sort of Google domination can obviously be extremely valuable for your business, so let's look at exactly how we did it.

The process began with a phone conversation I had with the client. He came to our tradesman marketing company as a plumbing company in need of a website, but before long the owner was talking passionately about helping elderly and disabled people stay in their own homes longer by building them walk in showers and baths. The level of service they were offering amazed me; they'd even take their customers out to the tile store to help them choose the tiles for their bath or shower! It was a great niche that made a real difference to people's lives.

One mistake a lot of plumbing companies make is assuming their customers know exactly what they do. For example, they assume that just because they install boilers, that if someone needs a boiler installed they know to call the plumber. This is the mistake that many businesses fall prey to. They focus on their *business* or *product* rather than the *solution* or *outcome* for the customer.

The end result is that there is a big fight for the keyword 'plumber' in every town, and the page is filled with plumbers who all appear completely generic and don't specialize in anything. Having talked to hundreds of plumbers I can tell you that every single one has a job that they prefer, or that they've become known for doing well. Why advertise every company as general plumbers when you can instead turn them into the specialist in their area and book them solid for their favourite type of job?

We decided to position the business as specialists in the installation of walk in showers and baths. We chose a domain name containing "walkinshowers" and optimised the entire site for the "walk in showers" and "walk in baths" phrases. Because this was a local business we added pages targeted at their locations, and set up linked Google+ Local pages.

Because we chose to narrow the focus of the site, it ranked extremely quickly and very prominently for all the target phrases. Google saw the site as extremely relevant (competitors might only use the phrase "walk in showers" once on their entire site), and the amount of content on the pages made prominent ranking a safe bet. The site had lots of pages targeted at different phrases and variations, which only boosted the relevance and authority of the site in Google's eyes: here is a site that is so precisely targeted to the topic of walk in showers and baths that its second most relevant page is still more likely to rank than their main target competitor.

Within 6 months, the site had the following rankings (due to the non-disclosure agreement we have removed the area name):

- 'walk in showers <area>': 4 of first 7 results
- 'walk in baths <area>': all 3 top results
- 'elderly baths <area>': all 4 top results
- 'elderly showers <area>': all 3 top results
- 'walk in showers <area 2>': all 3 top results
- 'walk in showers <area 3>': all top 4 results
- 'disabled baths <area>': all top 3 results
- 'disabled showers <area>': top result

As you can see, choosing a highly targeted keyword or phrase and building an entire website around it can produce fantastic results.

But we weren't finished there...

As part of the offsite promotion work, we listed the new website in some highly relevant local directories. These were chosen for their traffic as well as prominent ranking, and when creating the listings we optimised them to rank for our target phrases. The result of this optimisation was that these listings began to rank in Google in their own right. Why? These directory pages were better optimised for our target phrase than our client's competitors, so these listings outranked them.

Another useful tool in your multiple listings arsenal is video and, as we'll see elsewhere in this book, optimised video listings on sites like YouTube and Viddler can also rank on page 1 giving your business even more visibility over your competitors.

It can be tempting to copy text between two or more pages. For example, if you have a lot of geographic areas that you serve and you want to write about the identical products and services you offer at each area, it might seem that a nice little shortcut would be to copy all the text and just replace the name of the area. Job done!

Unfortunately, Google doesn't like duplicate text and actually punishes sites which contain a lot of duplicate text, whether it's text copied from other websites or text copied from other pages on the same website.

Just how different the text has to be in order to not be considered duplicate is a hot topic of discussion, but my advice would be to err on the side of caution and actually *write* different text for each page rather than going through changing a few words and reordering the odd sentence here and there. We know that Google generally only gets *tougher* on things it doesn't like, and it has displayed a dislike for duplicate text so just avoid it. Genuinely re-written text tends to read better than spun or reordered text anyway, and you might even find yourself explaining more clearly the second or third time around!

The neatest tool for identifying duplicate content is www.copyscape.com Their basic site allows you to identify if text on one page is duplicate, but by signing up for a premium account you can enter a list of all the pages on your site, or paste in a section of text to see if it exists elsewhere.

Image Optimisation

If you include pictures on your page, you'll have the option to set alt text – this is the text that shows up if the image doesn't load, or if someone uses software to read the page to them (if they are partially sighted, for example). The official line from Google doesn't exactly say "use your keywords as image alt text" but, to those of us who spend our lives reading between the lines of official Google statements, it certainly indicates that this is a good strategy. But as always, don't get too spammy.

Likewise when uploading pictures to your website, it's good practice to actually name the picture files something relevant to your Search Engine Optimisation. You don't want to get too spammy with this and just use your main keyword over and over again (remember that we're trying to avoid doing anything that looks unnatural), but "Omaha Hair Salon picture.jpg" is a better file name than "IMG00124.jpg".

Titles, Meta Descriptions and Meta Keywords

As well as the visible elements of your website (pages, content etc.) there is work that needs to be done behind the scenes in the code.

Page Titles

Word for word, Page Titles are the most important SEO element of your entire site. They indicate to Google (and visitors) which phrases you think the site should rank for. This title shows up in the visitor's browser tab and is shown by Google in the search results as the headline for your page. For these reasons, it's obviously important that your page titles are descriptive, appealing and include your target keywords.

In Google search results, anything longer than 57 characters will be truncated so if possible try to keep under this in order to control exactly what is shown to searchers.

To explain what makes a good Page Title, let's use an example of a site that was sent to us to review this morning that sells beautiful custom fitted kitchens in Exmouth, UK. Their current Homepage Title is set as:

Your Kitchen

```
<title>Your Kitchen</title>
```

That means this is what shows up in search results:

Your Kitchen ⟵————————————
www.yourkitchen.com/ ▾
We do more **fitted kitchens** in **Exmouth** - than anyone ! LEARN MORE >> · About Us · Wooden · Our Blog · White & Cream · Painted · High Gloss · Wooden · High ...
High Gloss - Our Blog - Find Us - Other Stuff

And in browser tabs:

| × | Your Kitchen | + |

Whilst this is their brand name, this is a terrible waste of a Page Title because it says nothing about the business and includes none of their target keywords. A much stronger Title would be:
Custom Fitted Kitchens in Exmouth | Your Kitchen

In this title we have their main target phrase, location and brand. This template can be used across the site and tweaked to be relevant for each page. For example, the page targeting Natural Wood Kitchens can use the title:
Fitted Wood Kitchens in Exmouth | Your Kitchen

Searchers that have just typed "Wood Kitchens Exmouth" into Google are going to be particularly tuned to that phrase so when they see the top result using those 3 words, that's going to lead to a higher Click Through Rate (CTR), solidifying ranking and bringing them more traffic.

Exactly how you go about changing your page title varies according to the platform your site is built on. If you're using Wordpress your Page Title is the main title in the Edit screen, although you'll usually want to use a different Meta title so that you can use a longer and more descriptive title without messing up your menus. By installing a plugin like All In One SEO Pack or SEO by Yoast you can specify Titles and Meta Descriptions for each of your pages without having to get involved with any code.

Likewise, Magento users can install an 'SEO Titles' plugin which will allow them to change their Page Titles without affecting the name of the page in menus and throughout the Magento backend.

Meta description

You'll remember the `<meta name="description"`... from our competitor analysis section. You might also remember that this is the descriptive text that sometimes shows up in the Google results, so is our chance to pitch potential website visitors on why they should click on our site rather than the completion. For that reason it's a good idea to make your Meta Description as enticing as possible, and of course you'll want to include your target keywords.

If you aren't the person responsible for building and maintaining your website, it might be tricky to change your Meta Description, and in fact this section is probably the most technical part of this entire book. It is possible to skip this section and still be OK, although taking care of this stuff does give you a bit of an edge.

As with Page Titles, if you are using Wordpress then editing your Meta Description is as simple as typing it into the All In One SEO Pack plugin fields on each page.

As with any of this stuff, if you are unsure how to change your Meta Descriptions in your particular website platform a quick Google search should give you the guidance you need.

So once you know *how* to change your Meta description, what should you write?

There are a few things to bear in mind when writing Meta descriptions:
1. You want it to be eye catching and trigger interest in potential customers, should they see it. Using boring generic text is never a good idea, so I'll sometimes include the first half of a testimonial in quotation marks so that people will be interested to find out the rest and click on the site. Stating your main benefit or compelling feature that stands you apart from your competition can also work well, for example "Free 24 hour Delivery".
2. Use your keywords by all means, but you really don't need to *stuff* your Meta description full of keywords, it's simply not necessary. Far more important is to get people to click on your site once they see it. Having said that, words matching the search phrase will show up bold in your meta

description on the Search engine results page, so it's definitely worth including them to demonstrate relevance and match what your searcher is looking for.

3. Google will only show 156 characters of your Meta description, so make sure that the important stuff is contained in the first 156 characters! There's little point writing a huge long Meta description, but used creatively the little '...' s that indicate the description carries on can be a useful source of intrigue for potential website visitors.

An example of a Meta description I might use for Sarah's Hair Salon could be something along the lines of:
Sarah's Hair Salon – beautifully cut hair in Weybridge. "My hair was so soft and shiny after my visit that my husband just couldn't wait and on the way home he..

At which point Google would chop off the Meta description and add the ... to signal read on. How many of Sarah's potential clients *wouldn't* click that website?

It goes without saying that the testimonials you use should always be true, and it's a good idea to include any that you use in the Meta Description on the page itself to satisfy those who want to find out how the story ended. You then have their attention on your page, and your website can get on with selling your service.

You will have noticed that when you search for a term in Google, any words or variations of those words that appear in the search results are highlighted in **bold**. This is a nice way to get attention as people are now conditioned that the bold writing is more relevant and they are more likely to click on a page that has a higher amount of bold writing in the title and description.

In the Sarah's hair description above, you'll notice that the word 'hair' is used 3 times, 'salon' is used, and 'Weybridge' also. The name 'Sarah's Hair Salon' is also in there as it's possible that people will be searching for Sarah's Hair Salon in particular. All of these words would be brought out in **bold**.

Meta Keywords

Many times, if you see a box allowing you to insert Meta Description and Title for your webpage you will also see a box for you to input 'Meta Keywords'. It is a nice idea that just by typing in the keywords we want to rank for Google will make us show up, but in reality Google ignores the Meta Keywords tag because it is so easy to manipulate. In the olden days of the Internet, Meta Keywords held more weight. Nowadays their biggest function is showing smart SEO-ers from your competition which keywords you have considered important and would like to rank for, saving them the time it takes to do the research for themselves.

We don't recommend spending any time adding Meta Keywords.

Rich Snippets: How to Make People Click On Your Website Even If It's Underneath Your Competitors

The beauty of having good Meta Descriptions and Page Titles is that they can bring you more visitors because they catch people's eyes – even if they appear below your competitors on the results page. There is another nice little trick we use whenever possible to make our clients' websites stand out on the results page.

You might have seen whilst surfing Google that some bigger directory websites have review stars next to their listings. They do this to stand out from the crowd and attract more clicks. From our own tests, it works. The downside is that Google can opt whether or not to show these stars in the search results - all we can do is set up the listings correctly and hope that Google decides to show them.

hReviews

Rich snippets are a name given to special text on a webpage that is accepted by Google to be information about a product or service and formatted in an agreed way. Examples of uses for rich snippets are business cards (so you can let Google know that your website is linked with a particular business), product details (this is why you sometimes see particular Amazon products show up in the listings, for example) and reviews (which is where these stars come from). There are many others, which are listed on the Schema.org website here https://schema.org/docs/gs.html#schemaorg_typ es but we are going to be concentrating on the reviews for now.

It's actually very straightforward to add reviews to your website, particularly if you are using Wordpress or another content management system.
What you have to remember is that people can get into trouble for adding fake reviews or reviews of themselves so it's always a good idea to have a hard copy of any reviews your customers make so that you could back yourself up, should your reviews' legitimacy ever come into question.

Anyway, with that out of the way let's look at how to add hReviews (what we call these review rich snippets) to your website.

If you're using Wordpress, simply go and download the free plugin *WP Customer Reviews*. This plugin allows you to include a button on each page of your website that your customers can click to add their review of your business, product or service. It's really that simple.

If you're using plain html, when you add a review or testimonial to your website, turning this into an hReview is simply a case of adding a bit more code.

This example is taken from the microformats.org website and shows a restaurant hReview:

```
<div class="hreview">
<span><span class="rating">5</span>
out of 5 stars</span>
<h4 class="summary">Crepes on Cole
is awesome</h4>
<span class="reviewer
vcard">Reviewer: <span
class="fn">Tantek</span> -    <abbr
class="dtreviewed"
title="20050418T2300-0700">April 18,
2005</abbr></span>
<div class="description item
vcard"><p>
<span class="fn org">Crepes on
Cole</span> is one of the best
little    creperies in <span
class="adr"><span
class="locality">San
Francisco</span></span>. Excellent
food and service. Plenty of tables
in a variety of sizes for parties
large and small.  Window seating
makes for excellent people watching
to/from the N-Judah which stops
right outside. I've had many fun
social gatherings here, as well as
gotten plenty of work done thanks to
neighborhood WiFi.</p></div>
<p>Visit date: <span>April
2005</span></p>
<p>Food eaten: <span>Florentine
crepe</span></p> </div>
```

If the sight of the above puts you off ever eating food again, then simply ask your web guy or gal to make sure your testimonials are hReviews. If they refuse or threaten to charge you lots of money, fire them, download Wordpress and install the WP Customer Reviews plugin instead.

If you look closely at the code above, you'll see that we have a number of different categories. In the first line you'll see `hReviews`, which simply tells Google's robots that this is, in fact, an hReviews.

In the next line we have the rating out of 5 stars. This rating is what shows up in the Google results. After that we have a short summary of the review, followed by the reviewer's name, then the date of the visit.

Then you have the description of the item, and included in this is the organization's name ("`fn org`") and location.

Not all of this info is necessary, and I personally only include the following fields in my clients' reviews:
- Name of reviewer: (customer in <area> if I don't know their name)
- Date of service/visit/purchase
- Rating (out of 5 stars)
- Review

Google can display your review stars in a couple different ways according to how you have your webpage set up.

If you have a page with loads of reviews from different people, then what Google will do is take an average star rating show this on the results page, along with some text like "from 6 reviews" or however many reviews you have on that page.

If you only have one review on that page, Google will just show that review along with the name of the reviewer.

Both methods are useful, and for some businesses I actually *prefer* to only have one review on most pages. Let's say that your website's homepage target keywords are 'electrician in Edinburgh'. You obviously also want to get some stars showing up with your homepage, but you probably don't want to devote half your homepage to all your most recent reviews, so what you can do instead is just include one review. Then instead of using the reviewer's name, you can use 'Customer in Edinburgh' (if they're actually from Edinburgh, of course).

That way, when someone searches 'electrician in Edinburgh' and sees your homepage in the results page, they will see the stars from your reviewer, plus the text "Customer in Edinburgh". MAJOR relevance here! Do you think that searcher is going to click on your site?

It's important that your website is structurally solid and there are no holes. By that I mean that there are no broken links, pages that don't exist or anything else that might look to a Google robot like your website is poor quality or broken. One good way to do this is through Google Webmaster tools, which we'll be looking at in more detail shortly, but it's also a good idea to check every link and button on each page to check they're all taking you to the right place and you're not getting any errors or 404 pages.

Website Speed

Your site's speed has a *significant* effect on its success. From an SEO perspective, Google rewards speedy sites with better ranking. In numerous cases we've seen a site get a significant ranking improvement after moving it to a faster server, with no other changes.

Website speed is not often talked about because it's a little bit technical and there's not usually much the business owner can do themselves other than demand from the tech team that they speed the website up. But it's just too important to ignore. The speed of your website has real, measurable effects on how profitable it is for you.

Mobile site speed

Where website speed is most important is on mobile devices. According to Google's Maile Ohye, the impact of a website taking an extra 1 second to load on a smartphone is a drop in page views of 9.4%. That's nearly 10% fewer pages being viewed on your site for just a 1 second increase. But it also hurts profit: the same additional second caused a 3.4% reduction in conversions. Internet users are impatient, and on mobile this impatience gets ramped up significantly.

Human Response Times: The 3 Important Limits

Jakob Neilsen's book *Usability Engineering* defines three time limits to be taken into consideration for all computer applications. Despite the fact that the book was published in 1993, the figures still hold true, as humans have not evolved significantly in 20 years.

- 0.1 second is the threshold for website users to feel that the site or application is responding to them in real time
- 1 second is the limit for the user's thought flow to stay uninterrupted. They'll notice the delay, but they'll approximately be in the same place they were when you left them.
- 10 seconds is the limit for keeping their attention. Thoughts will have wondered or they might start doing other things, so for delays as long or longer than 10 seconds we need to provide visual feedback to let them know when the site will be loaded.

So as you can see, 1-second page loading is the target to aim for so that we're keeping maximum engagement with the site.

According to a Kissmetrics study, 47% of web users expect a page to load within 2 seconds, and 40% of people abandon a site that takes longer than 3 seconds to load. They also claim that an additional second of loading hurts conversion rate by 7%. For a business bringing in £1,000 of enquiries per day, this 1-second will cost £25,000 each year.

Measuring your website's performance

There are a variety of free tools online to help you measure and diagnose any website speed issues you might have. The two we recommend most often are Google's Page Speed Insights (http://developers.google.com/speed/pagespeed/insights/) which highlights any potential issues and suggests solutions, and the Web Page Test (http://www.webpagetest.org/) which gives a 'waterfall' breakdown showing how long your site takes to load, and which elements are responsible for the delays.

While detailed technical instructions for speeding up every part of your site are beyond the scope of this book, here is our list of the most common problem areas:

- Leverage Browser Caching. Your website is made up of lots of different files, including images, CSS, HTML and JavaScript files. Not all of these files need to be downloaded every time someone revisits your site because many are unlikely to change from one day to the next. So to save time and bandwidth, browsers cache these files. Through your site's settings, you tell the browsers how often they need to 'refresh' these files, and obviously the longer the period between refreshes, the fewer downloads are required and the faster the page will reload. For Wordpress users, we recommend installing W3 Total Cache, which handles this automatically.

- Reduce Server Response Time. This indicates how long the server takes to respond to the request for the files. If the server is slow, the site is slow to load. Low budget hosting can be a cause of long response times, particularly if you're on a shared hosting plan.
- Optimise Images. Image files can usually be compressed without losing quality, and this means shorter download times. Wordpress users can use EWWW Image Optimizer to automatically optimise the images on their site.
- Prioritise visible content. If your website loads visible content first, this gives the illusion that the site has loaded quickly. By prioritising content that appears 'above the fold', you're giving your visitors a better experience and keeping them engaged. Again, the solution to this is quite technical but Google's Page Speed Service (currently

invite only, apply at https://developers.google.com/speed/pages peed/service) seeks to address this and some other issues automatically.

Another website speed factor is server location. If your site's visitors are half way across the world from your servers, any requests and transfers have to travel all that way, adding delay. By using servers located close to your audience, you can minimise this delay.

A neat service that helps in this area is Cloudflare. Cloudflare seeks to help optimise website speed in a number of ways, including through their optimizer and CDN (Content Delivery Network) which stores caches of your sites in each of its data centres around the world. When someone visits your site, the files are sent from the closest data centre, saving them from having to travel across the world. Cloudflare is free for basic accounts, and relatively easy to set up, so it's definitely worth a look.

Increasing website speed is too important to ignore but for most business owners addressing these sort of issues themselves is an ineffective and unprofitable use of time. If it's possible to implement the suggestions here for a cost, it's usually worth it.

Submitting Your Site to Google and Monitoring Progress

Once you've built your sitemap and optimised your site's content, the next step is to link it through Webmaster Tools.

Go to www.google.com/webmasters and follow the sign up process to create your Webmaster Tools account. Once you've done this you'll see an option to Add A Site. Enter your site's URL and follow the instructions verify ownership of your website.

Once you've verified ownership of your website you'll want to submit your sitemap. In your main Webmaster dashboard you'll see a section called Sitemaps. By clicking on the heading you'll see a button that says Add/Test Sitemap. Drop in the URL of your sitemap and click Submit sitemap. After a couple of seconds you'll see an option to refresh the page and this should show you that your sitemap has been successfully submitted.

The next step is to submit your site to Google's index. In Webmaster Tools you should see a menu on the left hand side of the page. Click Crawl to expand the menu and choose the Fetch as Google option. Once the page loads you'll see your site's URL with a red box that says Fetch. Click this box and you'll see a button titled Submit to index appear. Click this and you'll get the option to submit your site to Google's index. Choose the *URL and all linked pages* option to submit your entire site (rather than just the homepage) to the index. Simple!

Google+ Integration

Authorship Markup

Previous editions of this book explained how to add Authorship Markup in order to get your face showing up next to your website in search results. However, Google abandoned this feature in 2014 so it no longer makes sense to bother coding it into your website.

Google+ Business Integration

For businesses, Google+ comes in two flavours: Google+ Local and Google+ Business

Google+ Local is Google's business listing platform that also feeds the maps results you see for local searches, whilst Google+ Business is designed for brands and companies for whom physical location is not important.

The main thing to note about Google+ Business is that it's a *total freakin' mess*. It's complicated and can take a long time to get the page setup and verified. And trying to get your customers to leave reviews on your page is going to get you struck of many a Christmas card list because it's *such* a ball ache.

Unfortunately the benefits still outweigh the considerable pain for business owners trying to get to grips with Google+. All we can hope for is that the platform settles down and becomes a bit more user-friendly.

The main reasons that Google+ is a massive MUST for local businesses are:
• The inclusion of big, eye catching address blocks for certain Google+ Local associated websites, and large Google+ blocks for non-local businesses
• A presence on the Google map
• If the searcher is signed in to Google+ and their friends like your page, this will show in the search results and make your page more likely to show up (this is Google's 'Search Plus Your World' – their attempt to make personalized and more relevant search results for Google+ users).

To get these benefits you'll need to link your website to your business's Google+ Local page, creating that page first if it doesn't already exist.

Go to www.google.com/business and follow the instructions to set up your business page. The first thing you'll do is search Google's database for any existing listings that match your business, then you can go through the process of setting up and optimising your profile.

As with any online listing, you'll want to add as much information as you can to make your profile as complete as possible. In your description aim for at least 300 words and include your main keywords, USPs and background on the company. Remember that you can include links back to pages on your website and it's good practice to do this when mentioning specific services or product

122

categories that you offer so that anyone finding your Google+ page can go directly to the page that interests them.

Upload as many pictures and videos as you can, as Google is more likely to show a complete profile than one that makes Google+ look like a seldom-used failure (ahem!).

One of the most important tasks is linking your website and Google+ page. This is easiest if you have a Google Webmasters account that the site is verified through, as you can simply request that the site and Google+ property are linked. In Webmaster tools you'll see a notification and will be able to approve this request.

If you don't, then you'll need to add a snippet of code to your website (usually we put it in the footer) which just tells Google that the properties are linked.

If you are claiming your page for the first time, Google will likely send out a postcode with a PIN number to verify that you are in fact the owner of the premises and not a sneaky competitor trying to claim your Google+ page.

Now you play the Google+ waiting game as you wait to find out when and how much of this new Google+ information will show up in the search results.

Google+ Reviews

One of the strategies that can really set you apart as a local business is the collection of Google+ reviews:

Epsom Dental Centre
epsomdental.co.uk
4.6 ★★★★★ 8 Google reviews · Google+ page

Ⓑ 37 Waterloo Road
Epsom
01372 720650

These reviews make your listing stand out in the map results and improve your listing's visibility. There's a five-review threshold that you need to cross to get the star rating displayed, so you need to be on the case giving your customers instructions for leaving their reviews. They'll need to be signed up to Google+, which will inevitably put many off, but remember that this is a blessing in disguise as many of your competitors simply won't bother with collecting reviews because it's too much effort.

Something that lots of people ask at this point is about how easy it is to fake reviews on Google+. While it's certainly possible, Google is extremely savvy with tracking the IP addresses and individual computers that people sign in from in order to leave their reviews. The guidelines are extremely strict and technically it's forbidden to even solicit reviews. If there's any suspicion about the validity of the reviews, they'll disappear (along with legitimate reviews, in many cases). To make matters worse, if you start getting reviews very quickly you might find some of them disappear. If you get lots of new Google+ users leaving reviews, again they can just disappear. Despite all of this, persuading your customers to leave reviews on Google+ is just one of those things that you need to do.

Promoting Your Website Elsewhere

Once you have your website set up and fully readable by Google, it's time to get promoting it online. Promotion is an incredibly important part of getting your website to the top of Google, because websites that have lots of good quality links pointing at them are much easier to rank. Websites with few or no links pointing at them are unlikely to rank, because Google sees them as less authoritative.

We talked a bit about PageRank earlier in the book and how PageRank 'flows' to the sites that are linked from that web page. The ideal scenario is that you get lots of juicy links to your site from websites that have high PageRank and are extremely relevant to your topic and market.

How to Show Up On The First Page Of Google Using Other People's Websites

The quickest and easiest source of links for many businesses is directory websites. There are a whole host of free and paid options out there, and the best choices for you depend on your market and type of business.

Having your website listed in lots of directories is useful for three reasons:

1. The links from the directories back to your website will give your website more authority in Google's eyes, and push it up the rankings
2. If the directories are high quality and loved by Google (these are the best sort) and your entries are well optimized, then these entries themselves might start ranking high on Google. This is the case with Yelp.com, for example, which is currently a bit of a Google darling. It's typical in the US for Google searches for local businesses to list Yelp listings in the top 3-5 positions, for example.
3. Potential customers who somehow end up on the directory website might find your listing and give you a call. However, don't let the directory website blurb fool you – according to our extensive experience with dozens of clients and their directory listings, this is relatively uncommon.

You'll notice that most free directory websites offer a paid membership, which usually involves promise of more exposure and being listed at the top of searches for your category. If you really want to test this, feel free. But primarily we are using the directories for their Google juice and not the traffic that is already using the directory website, in which case a free listing is adequate.

Whatever business you are in, here are some ways to maximize your Google ranking with your listings:
- Be sure to use your business name in the title, but also the main keyword you are

targeting. For example "Matt The Builder – Extension building specialist serving Kent and East Sussex"

- In the description, be sure to use your keywords plenty of times, but make the description readable for humans too – you never know, this listing might rank above your own website for a while so think about what your potential customers would want to read in order to get in contact with you
- If the directory allows it, add links to your website in the description and use relevant keywords as anchor text (for example your link might look like this: <a href="http://mattthebuilder.com">Extensions Builder in Kent</a>, and would show up on the page as Extensions Builder in Kent. While most directories automatically add nofollow to your links (meaning that you don't get PageRank from the link), they don't *all* add nofollow so if in doubt, add a link.
- Make sure your contact details are *exactly* the same as any contact details you use in your Google+ local listing and on your website, if relevant. This then forms what's known as a 'citation', and citations contribute to boosting the ranking of Google+ Local pages.
- If the directory gives you the option to add pictures and/or videos, opening hours, payment options etc., add these. Every directory wants its listings to look fully kitted-out and many will reward listings that have been filled out completely with higher ranking on their sites. It also converts more

visitors and makes you stand out from the dozens/hundreds/thousands of other generic listings that will likely make up the bulk of the directory.

Market-specific directories vs. General directories

Whatever business you are in there will usually be online directories that are targeted specifically for your market. If you are a local business serving customers in one particular area, you will also find that there are local directories for your area.

In general, these highly targeted directories are a very good idea. Google gives additional weight to links from targeted and relevant websites, although good quality general links also help. It's also more likely that visitors to niche directories will more likely be potential customers for you as they have already narrowed themselves down either geographically or by interest to be on the site in the first place.

The method I use to find new good quality directories for a business is to Google each of the keywords I'm targeting, and look for directory listings in the results. If a directory site is ranking prominently on Google, then it's a safe bet to say it's considered to be good quality. When I find a directory page, I'll add it to the list of directories to submit to.

While using the Backlinkwatch and Open Site Explorer tools mentioned earlier you might also notice that your high-ranking competitors are listed in certain directories and these will make good additions to your directory list.

Adding Too Many Listings At Once

There has been plenty of talk online of Google 'punishing' websites who seem to get unnatural numbers of links all in a short period of time. The reasoning is that this appears like spammy behaviour, or an obvious attempt at manipulating Google's rankings. While the argument about the logic behind this theory is something completely separate, it's somewhat irrelevant to our plan. The beauty of most of the directories you will find is that your entry requires some sort of manual approval.

This approval can take minutes, hours, days, weeks or even months. So adding your website to fifty directories over the course of a day won't create 50 directory profiles instantly, but your exposure will be more spread out over time. Even if adding your site to fifty directories in a day did create 50 profiles instantly, Google would take some time to crawl these directories and add your listing to its index, so there's really no need to worry about it.

As with any repetitive online task, it can be tempting to wonder about a software solution to get all these directory listings taken care of.

The advantage of creating directory listings manually is that you get a greater level of acceptance. Directories tend to favour manual submission and many will reject automatic submission instantly, and might even ban you from submitting again.

Then there is accuracy. Obviously when you are in charge of adding your listing, you are going to be in the right category and with all your details in the right place.

Automatic submission doesn't offer this level of accuracy but it does offer significant timesaving if you are responsible for submitting lots of different sites to a number of directories. If you are just optimizing the one website, then even setting up the automatic submission could take a long time.

We use and recommend manual submission all the time. If your time is too valuable to sit and manually submit your business info to dozens of quality directories, then outsource it. But it needs to be done.

There are plenty of services out there offering directory submission. While some services can seem extremely cheap, they will often use automatic submission, exactly the same description each time (and could therefore be flagged by Google as duplicate content) and submit to poor quality directories (which could harm your Google rank). The best quality directories require manual submission, verification by email and tend to be avoided by cheap auto submission services.

Also remember that with any directory submission service, the advertised number of submissions will tend to be far higher than the number of listings you will actually receive, as many directories will reject the submitted listing for whatever reason.

So what to do? If you have the time do your own directory listing. Yes it's boring, but it's worth doing well.

If you really can't face it, get in touch with Exposure Ninja as our SEO Ninjas actually *enjoy* finding and listing in the best directories for each market.

SEO/PR

The best way we've found to get high quality links to a website is through our own combination of SEO and Online PR. SEO/PR (as we call it) not only gives your website high quality and authority links, but also raises the profile of your business (and you or your figurehead) in your industry and leads to increased custom.

Use PR as Free Advertising

PR is something that many business owners dismiss until they are in 'the big leagues', usually for two reasons:
1. Their image of PR is breakfast television interviews and national newspaper coverage. As a result, they assume it's out of reach.
2. They associate it with highly paid traditional PRs, networking over coffees and inhabiting an impenetrable world of relationships. Without these relationships, it seems impossible to 'break in'.

Unfortunately these assumptions hold back countless businesses. It's a tragedy.

The truth about PR is quite different:
1. It can be very easy to get coverage in a variety of different channels.
2. Savvy businesses can do this for little or no cost at all.

Every day, editors of publications in every perceivable subject area stare at half empty computer screens wondering how they are going to fill their next issue with good content. Worse, once they finish this month's magazine, today's show or this week's blog posts, the page becomes blank again and they must start from scratch. With shrinking budgets, tight deadlines and a readership with more choice and distraction than ever, the pressure these poor editors face is immense.

This is where you, the savvy business owner, come in: the editor's friend and knight in shining armour. Armed with fascinating insights into your industry, current trends and customers' needs, you provide the tired stressed editor with exactly what they want: quality content of interest to their audience. They thank you from the bottom of their heart and tell you that you're welcome back any time to save their bacon again.

If this sounds like a wishful fantasy, think again. The perception that PR is a dark magic art, impossible for those 'outside the loop' is a creation of those who have either never attempted it, or who don't approach it with the right mindset.

The reality is that it's surprisingly easy to get promotional content published, free of charge, in most publications. But the key is to treat it as any other sales job. There is a customer (the editor or journalist) to whom you want to sell your product (your story). You sell to a customer by explaining and demonstrating how your product or service meets their needs, and the process of securing press coverage should be exactly the same.

Once you understand your customer's unmet need, you can create something of value to them and make the sale. Their need in this situation is to provide their readers, viewers or subscribers with useful or interesting content in order to increase the likelihood that they'll read, watch or continue their subscription. If you can help them meet this need by providing the useful or interesting information they're after, they will gladly use it.

The approach that *doesn't* work so well is the typical PR approach used by most companies who dabble. They publish press releases with titles like "Company X announces product Y. Now 12% faster and with faster response time..." Boring, overly promotional, valueless drivel, and nobody cares. Even if you manage to find an editor that will print this type of thing, it doesn't get read and it certainly doesn't generate much excitement or interest amongst readers (your ultimate target audience).

Obviously the most effective ads focus on the customer and the *benefits* of your product or service, and a press release or article should be no different. The stories with the highest chance of publication are those that provide a new insight, recommendations or advice for readers or viewers, a timely survey or perhaps analysis on something current.

We're not saying you can't talk about your new product or service. Of course there should be a self-promotional component, otherwise we are simply freelance writers or interviewees working for free. But there has to be an angle that is of interest to the audience in order to get the story published and read.

For first time PR writers, it can be difficult to find an angle for your story that will be interesting and relevant to your target audience. Here are some questions that we use early on working with clients:

- Have you noticed a particular trend in their buying patterns (fashion)?
- Do you have some recommendations for them to avoid some common mistakes, thus positioning your business as the helpful expert?
- If you are announcing a new product, service or business, what sort of interesting stories can you tell about why you are launching it?
- Is there a large unmet need that you seek to meet, or is there something that places you perfectly to help a particular type of customer?
- Do you personally have a story that others would find motivational or inspirational? Careful with this one though - you've

probably noticed that our own stories can be disproportionately fascinating to ourselves.

Once you have chosen your angle, it's time to do some outreach. Whenever we are getting an article or news item published, we'll draw up a list of suitable outlets and pitch them a slightly different variation of the idea. This allows us to offer each of them exclusivity on that particular story, which dramatically increases the likelihood of it being placed. We'll research and contact the most suitable person - usually by email, sometimes by phone - offering the story and asking if they think it would be of interest to their readers.

If you have an attractive angle and the editor can see how the readers would find your story interesting, you'll often get a positive response asking you to send over the article. This is when you write the article and send it over. We've found this two-step approach to be much more effective than sending the article cold. The offer of exclusivity is also a differentiator as these folk are used to being blasted an email with 100 other poorly selected contacts in the CC: line.

Once an editor has requested your article, do the work properly and prepare it in a way that fits with the style of the publication. Use a similar word count and language to other published articles so that minimal editing is required. If you send over a half-finished piece that requires extensive rewriting, it's far less appealing than a ready to publish finished article. If it needs to be proof read, then hire a proofreader. Give it your very best shot and work as if it really matters. Trust us, it won't go unnoticed with the editor.

If you're writing for a magazine or newspaper, try to include an image that they can use alongside the story. Where possible it should be original, because this eliminates any copyright or licensing issues. If you have to use a stock photo, be careful to explain to the editor exactly where you got the photo from and, if possible, link them to the terms of the license. Again the aim is to make publishing your article an extremely simple and desirable proposition. The more work you require the publication to do (including sourcing a suitable picture), the more you decrease the likelihood of them running the piece.

You'll obviously want to include an element of promotion in your article, and you can approach this in two ways (This section is taken from my book 101 Ways to Get More Customers, and while it's not strictly SEO-related, it is *very* profitable so I wanted to include it here):

Free Advertising/Lead Generation

We have built two entire businesses on the back of lead generation campaigns run through articles written for magazines. The articles provide insight or advice about a particular subject of interest to the reader, and then offer a free gift to readers. They are invited to text or visit a website to claim their free gift, and we then use these contact details to market to them. The free gift itself is usually a piece of promotional material with enough valuable information contained in it for it to have high-perceived value.

By using press in this way, we're essentially getting highly effective advertising, free of charge and disguised as articles. The quality of the articles is so high that they attract readers, and by offering a tantalising offer at the end we're making sure that we motivate the readers to action (giving us their contact details).

Of course, some publications will smell a rat with this approach and see that you're just sneaking in some free advertising under the radar. Most won't though, and they'll happily run your ads free of charge.

For those that do protest at your inclusion of an offer, you can strike a deal to run a paid advert as well, in return for the article's inclusion. Don't fall for the 'minimum of 5 insertions' rule to 'build familiarity', but instead tell the magazine that you're testing the effectiveness of the ad using a lead generation offer, so you'll immediately be able to gauge the response rate.

Positioning and Awareness

The softer approach to running a lead generation press campaign is to try and build awareness of your product or service with the hope that readers or viewers will take action on their own accord to become customers. While this is much easier than designing and running a lead generation campaign, it's also generally much less effective and will generate far fewer direct customers.

Pitching for TV Coverage

If you're aiming for TV or online video coverage, do everything you can to show your contact that you'd make a good interviewee. Send a short and well-lit video of yourself in front of the camera appearing comfortable and relaxed. Make sure you know what you're going to be saying, and your lines are well enough rehearsed that they sound natural and you can focus more on the delivery than what you're actually saying. To make the most of any TV appearances you get, make sure to do whatever you can to get a link from the show's website as the authority and quality of these sites tends to be very good.

Follow up

The folks receiving articles and emails for press coverage tend to be extremely busy and deluged with emails, so it's a good idea to send a follow up after a couple of working days if you haven't heard back from them. Politely ask if they received your work, and if they had any feedback as to whether it would be the sort of thing their audience would be interested in. We find that it's almost *always* only through the follow up that we get a response from the editor, so it's important to be diligent about it.

Thank anyone who offers to run the piece and remember to ask for a copy of the publication. Your appearance in recognised publications is useful to put on your website and use in your marketing as a credibility tool, so remember to blog and tweet about it once it's live.

SEO/PR and Backlinks

Most of the print publications you might be targeting as part of your PR campaign will either be online or, if they're a traditional magazine or newspaper, they'll have an online counterpart, whether it's a full online version of the print magazine or a companion website. Most of the time, these counterpart websites or online publications still get a fraction of the readership of the print versions, but they have very high authority and relevance, so links from these sites are SEO gold.
Likewise, online-only publications such as niche blogs or magazine-type sites can be extremely targeted and give huge SEO benefits through links back to your website.

So let's say that you've pitched an article to a publication in your market, the editor has agreed and you've had created an awesome article that matches the style of the publication. How do you turn this into good SEO?

The best way to do this is include a subtle and relevant link or two in the body of the article at a relevant time. Typically, the sort of articles that we'll pitch for a holiday company could be '5 Perfect UK Getaway Destinations'. What we'll then do is link to five *separate* websites, with the other 4 being higher PageRank sites than our client's - if possible, significantly higher. This demonstrates to Google that the company the site keeps is very high.

Finding Additional PR Opportunities Online

There are plenty of places that businesses looking to generate press can go online to find such opportunities. Every day, busy and overworked journalists and editors are trying to fill their publications and find interviewees to beef up their articles. This type of promotion is on so few of your competitors' radars that it can be incredibly easy to secure it.

Journalist enquiry services (also called media enquiry services) are services that journalists use to put out requests for businesses and PRs to talk to or interview for their articles or TV features. Subscribers (and there is usually a cost for the best quality services) receive notifications by email of any enquiries that come in matching the criteria they have selected.

Let's look at an example:

Kate runs a shop that sells boutique lighting, and she wants to promote her e-commerce store through some well-targeted press exposure. She subscribes to a media enquiry service and chooses the Interiors and Home category, indicating the type of enquiry that she is interested in.

She then starts to receive requests from journalists looking for businesses that can provide content, including one from a TV production company looking for products to feature in a home renovations show - the sort of enquiry that is fairly typical in this type of category. Kate responds and finds out that she would need to provide any products free of charge, but that they would be featured on the TV show's website and her company's website would be appear briefly on the show. She decides that for the cost of the lights this is a great investment.

For the cost of the lighting, Kate has secured:
• Placement in a TV show
• A link to her e-commerce store from the TV show website
• Positioning of her products in front of a qualified target audience (those interested in interior design)

How else can Kate take advantage? As her lighting has appeared on the TV show, she can now use the channel and TV show's logos on her website. This boosts her store's credibility and increases trust amongst visitors new to the site. If Kate wants to leverage the appearance still further, she can use the story of appearing on the show in other publications, for example local newspapers. Local newspapers are so desperate for content that, with a good angle, she stands a good chance of getting some coverage in a 'local girl done good' type of piece.

Industry Magazines and Blogs

You'd be amazed at how easy it can be to get a regular, high visible 'guest' blog on high profile magazine websites in your industry. Every market has them, whether they're online only or the website companion to the most popular magazines.

Every blog editor knows that they need plenty of good quality content for their blog, and they also know that paying their own team to write it is expensive. Worse, it's not always easy to get really good quality content 'straight from the frontline'. Professional writers are usually a little insulated from the action, and yet they are expected to be the fountain of knowledge to an audience made up of the *real* experts. You, on the other hand, are well positioned to offer a unique perspective on your industry, and if you show that you're sympathetic to the writing style and target audience, you can quickly become the blog editor's best friend.

So how do you go about securing a regular blog?

The first step is outreach, just as it is with securing a single article. In fact we usually recommend offering just a single article to begin with, because you're more likely to secure the regular blog one you've shown the editor that you can work quickly and your writing is of a good standard. Once they've published the article, it's important to thank them and mention what sort of response you've had from the blog audience (clue: it's best to let them know the response was "unbelievable", even if it was unbelievably *disappointing*). This is the best time to suggest that you write a follow up piece, and to hint that perhaps you could look at making it a more regular blog as you have plenty to offer on the subject.

If they agree, they might suggest that you submit pieces at a certain interval. Left to its own devices this interval will invariably grow wider and wider as time goes on, so if at all possible stick it in the calendar and book an appointment with yourself to write your blog post each month.

As with any PR outreach attempts, the key is volume. If you rely on contacting only one site, you'll probably be disappointed when they don't reply. If you set a goal to contact 5-10 sites, you're much more likely to get at least one of them agree. Do this once a week and you'll have the basis of a good link acquisition strategy.

Finding PR opportunities online is on-going work that you can do in the background of your online social life. Each time you find a relevant publication or blog, drop them a line and keep a note of it in a press schedule. We find that a simple spreadsheet with the name of the publication, key contact, date of first contact, date of follow ups and date of expected publication (once they've agreed) allows you to keep your press exposure organised. It's a useful tool allowing you to schedule your different promotions through the quarter so you're not hit by an unexpected spike in demand.

The opportunities are out there, and the vast majority of your competitors are doing absolutely nothing about them. Don't be one of them, and make sure that you have an online-PR component in your 2015 marketing plan.

A good place for local businesses to get articles published is, believe it or not, your local newspaper's website. They are often pretty desperate for content and a quick article on helping your town's residents decide what haircut to get, hot new property trends in 2015, fashionable uses for single-storey extensions etc. can be something of real interest to local people. These sites are also more likely to allow you to link to your website and again provide targeted traffic which can lead to real business and, again, often an email or phone call to the news desk editor will be sufficient to get your article online.

Many business owners new to SEO/PR struggle with a subject for their article, but a quick browse of local newspaper story subjects should put your mind at ease: often there isn't a whole lot going on to write about! A story about the new website being unveiled may or may not be of sufficient interest to their readers to get a decent sized article in, but a story about a reader-exclusive offer might. Stories about celebrities or quasi-celebrities make good subject matter, and if you have any interaction with anybody who is even slightly famous during the running of your business, be sure to grab a picture with them or get a testimonial as the power this has is immense.

Duplicate Content

We talked about Google's stance on duplicate content (clue: it doesn't like it) at various points in this book, and unsurprisingly duplicate content in published articles or directories is another no-no (with the exception of listings of your name, address and phone number which should always be precisely duplicated).

One of the most common ways grey or black hat SEOs use to create duplicate content online is to use article 'spinners'. Spinners change the content of articles while aiming to keep the overall message the same. For example changing "Sarah's Salon has been trading to local customers in Weybridge since 2011" to "Sarah's Salon has been selling to nearby clients in Weybridge since 2011".

The content of the sentences is nearly identical, and the level of spinning is adjustable allowing thousands of different variations of each sentence. While this can seem appealing to try and get past Google's tough stance on duplicate content, our position is and has always been:

Google knows about spinning. Websites with spun content tend to be full of spam. Google is constantly working to rid its search results of websites full of spam. Therefore, even if you can get away with spun content now, it's unlikely that this shortcut will remain for much longer.

Again, the alternative is more time consuming and laborious but produces far better results, and that is to manually rewrite any content that you need to 'duplicate' anywhere online - whether it's your website or microsite, external articles or blog posts, or business listing descriptions. It takes time but means that you can be sure your entries won't get flagged for duplicate content and also that any potential customers who stumble across your entry won't be put off by a spammy vibe (you can *always* tell spun content – you might have seen blog comments that have been spun so far they make absolutely no sense whatsoever).

E-Commerce and Duplicate Content

One of the most common SEO issues for E-commerce sites is a lack of original content on product pages. This is a particular issue for affiliate sites or 'pre built' E-com projects that already include product descriptions. In these cases, the content might be shared between dozens or even hundreds of sites across the Internet and in the worst scenarios there can be no original content on the entire site. One of the most important things that E-commerce sites can do to boost their quality in Google's eyes is to include plenty of original writing on all product and category pages.

Work out what you can do to make each of your product pages *the most useful* page selling that product anywhere online, as this will give Google the justification to rank your site prominently.

Similarly if your category pages contain no text content, the best thing you can do is to figure out how to add some good quality text - even if it's only a couple of hundred words - as these category pages are often the pages that Google would typically choose to rank. Text on category pages can help visitors to decide which products will best meet their needs or introduce the various brands that create the products in that category.

Customer Reviews for Content

Another neat way to get the product pages stuffed full of good quality content is to build customer reviews into your follow-up strategy. Part of the reason Amazon's pages always rank so well is the customer reviews on every page offer a lot of unique, highly-relevant content about every product in their store. The truly genius part is that all of this content is user-generated, so Amazon no longer has to spend on editorial talent to flesh out these pages.

By implementing customer review functionality on your site and gently reminding buyers to leave a review, you can put a large portion of your content generation strategy on autopilot.

Be Careful of Spammy Sites

In its Panda Update, Google started punishing low quality sites designed purely to trick visitors into viewing them and get high rankings in Google. The sort of sites that have been affected are those annoying sites that show up looking really relevant until you click on them to find they're just a pile of automatically generated content or directory listings.

What's more, Google is now not only punishing these sites, but also punishing sites that these sites *link to.* Google Webmaster tools now warns webmasters when a number of low quality websites are linking to them, and suggests that they go through and get these links removed. This is pretty annoying if you have thousands of links from crappy websites like these!

What this means is that many websites that relied on lots of low quality backlinks from these spam sites started plummeting down the rankings.

The SEO companies that had been using these strategies were forced to change their game plan literally overnight in order to get their websites back up in the rankings, and the fallout has been huge. Much of the cheap SEO industry was wiped out because they just couldn't make enough profit on the high-effort strategies that boosted Google ranking compared to the cheap spam that used to work. Incidentally this worked out very nicely for Exposure Ninja, as we've never used the sort of strategies that get sites hit by penalties. So while most of our 'competitors' were scrambling to adjust or going bust, we were taking their clients and recovering their ranking through good quality SEO.

But for the sake of boosting Google ranking, low quality websites designed purely for link building are totally dead. This is another reason to avoid automatic submission or outsourcing to less than scrupulous companies who have no regard for the quality of sites that they submit their clients addresses to, as you have little assurance that you won't end up being associated with one of these spam hangouts, and your site's rankings dragged down as a result.

Penguin Penalties and Recovery

Every time a new Google update rolls out, the ninja phone and inbox is barraged with requests for help from website owners who have been negatively affected. As well as keeping us out of mischief, this also gives us a nice opportunity to see exactly which sites are getting penalised, and how to recover the penalties.

Each Penguin algorithm change focuses on the same thing: low quality inbound links. Subsequent updates simply refine the meaning of *low quality* and add new data that Google has collected since the previous update into the mix. When your ranking is impacted by a Penguin update it means that Google has caught up with low quality links that have been created in the past, or re-categorised 'grey area' links as spam. We'll look at algorithmic penalties and how to recover from them in just a minute, but first I want to discuss manual penalties.

Manual Penalties

Manual penalties are levied by one of Google's (human) web spam team. They are given for spamming behaviour that is brought to the attention of the team or noticed while they conduct their everyday Internet trawling. As the name suggests, these penalties are manually slapped onto a site and their effect can be large or medium-sized. When your site is hit by a manual penalty Google will usually tell you through Webmaster tools. This could be in the form of an 'unnatural link notice' or another message which basically says "you're doing something wrong".

In order to recover from a manual penalty, you need to fix the issue mentioned in the penalty notice and have someone from Google manually remove the penalty. Usually this involves fixing dodgy links or otherwise removing the 'forbidden' SEO that you've been doing. Once you've done this, you'll need to file a Reconsideration Request through Webmaster tools detailing what you've done to fix it and that you're very *very* sorry for your sins.

In some cases, it's not always obvious what the manual penalty might be for. If this is the case, good luck trying to get any further information from Google! Luckily you can head to the Google Webmaster forums and explain your case there, helpful SEOs will pitch in and advise you on possible causes and how to correct them. Alternatively drop us an email through the Exposure Ninja website and help you identify the cause of the ranking drop.

Algorithmic Penalties

Unlike a manual penalty, an algorithmic penalty hasn't been applied by someone at Google. They're applied automatically as a result of updates to the equations Google uses to decide ranking.

This means that (usually) once you fix the underlying cause of the penalty, the penalty will no longer apply. Think of it like a printer jam – once you remove the screwed up paper being mashed by the rollers, the printer will resume printing as it was before the jam occurred.

So that's the good news. The bad news is that removing the jam usually requires a fair bit of work (much like undoing the action that caused a manual penalty). The other bad news is that once you remove the offending backlinks, it could still take a while before your site is performing how it used to be in the search results. Google's John Mueller stated recently that the time between fixing the cause of an algorithmic penalty and the effects of the penalty being completely lifted could be as long as a year, although in our experience it's usually much quicker. I'll give you some example case studies of penalty recoveries later in this chapter.

Removing Spammy Backlinks

The commonality between recovery from manual and algorithmic penalties is that they can both involve having to remove spammy backlinks. The bad old days of *10,000 backlinks for $5* are not only over, but they're resurfacing to haunt the site owners that revelled in them. Those 10,000 links may no longer all be live, but the ones that are now should be removed. Unfortunately, removing them is going to take a fair amount more work than creating them did however.

But before we even get to removal of spammy backlinks, let's address how to identify a spammy backlink compared to a regular, quality backlink.
The first step in this process is to sign into Google Webmaster Tools. If you've jumped straight to this section and your site isn't already registered with WMT, then go to google.com/webmasters and sign up. Once in, you'll need to go through the instructions to add your site.

Once your site is added, you'll see a menu down the left hand side of the screen that includes a heading titled Traffic. Click on this to expand and you'll see an option "Links to your site".

This section gives an indication of the links Google is 'seeing' pointing to your site. There's no guarantee that this is comprehensive (Google never tells you everything it knows), but this list of sites back linking you is what we'll be using to eliminate the cause of any manual or algorithmic penalty resulting from spammy links.

Once you have this list, you'll need to go through each of the links to see if the site is
1. Relevant to your market, niche, location or subject
2. Good quality and user-focussed

In most cases, it's pretty easy to tell if a link is going to be relevant simply from the domain name of the site. But if you're struggling, here are some pretty good guidelines for spotting spammy sites:

- If the site name has 'SEO' in it, for example www.seo-article-submission.com, it's usually junk
- If the site looks to be a regular blog site but each of the posts has loads of spammy junky comments, all with backlinks and all completely irrelevant to the subject of the post
- If the page linked actually doesn't contain a backlink to your site, but does contain other backlinks to sites that aren't relevant

For each of the spammy linked sites, copy the URL of the domain (not just the page URL) into a text file on a new line. This text file will form the basis of your link removal work.

Once you've been through all the URLs and picked out the potentially spammy sites, you'll need to contact the owners of these sites requesting removal of your links.

The best way to do this is to send a polite email to the email address of the site owner, or any other email address you can find on the site. This email should state that you are trying to recover from a Google penalty and you'd appreciate if the site owner would remove the link back to your site.

It's best not to imply that the site you are contacting has anything to do with the penalty, and we usually include a line along the lines of "Please note I am not questioning your site's integrity or quality at all, we're just trying to remove as many links as possible". Remember that we're essentially asking the site owner for a favour, so it pays to be polite and avoid threats or aggression in the tone of the email.

If you can't find an email address on the site, you can usually get contact details of the domain owner from who.is.

Once you've contacted the site owners requesting removal of the links, make a note of this in your text document. This could be quite a long process if you have a lot of links!

What will happen now depends on each site owner. Some will remove links, some will get nasty and some you will never hear from. Thank those that remove the links, be calm and polite with the ones that get nasty and gently remind those who don't reply. The nasty responses are generally along the lines of 'but it was YOU who put these links on my site in the first place, why should it be MY problem to get them removed?' Well, they've got a point! In which case we let them know that we completely understand their point of view, but that we weren't the company responsible for the links (the previous SEOs responsible for the bad linking were usually fired long ago) and our client is really suffering from the Google Penalty.

Not all site owners will remove the links. Depending on the sites you contact, you'll probably find that most don't. The important thing is that you try and make a record of your attempts, as it'll help your case with Google if you can demonstrate that you've had a go at removing the bad links manually.

The Disavow Tool

Once you've removed as many of the bad links as you can, you'll need to submit the remaining sites to the disavow tool inside Webmaster Tools. This tells Google to ignore links from these sites as you've recognised they're spammy and you don't want your site to be associated with them.

To do this, open your text document with the domains listed and the results of your link removal requests. Delete the sites that you've successfully removed links from and include comments detailing your attempts to remove the links from the remaining domains, such as the following (taken from Google's own documentation):

```
# example.com removed most links,
but missed these
http://spam.example.com/stuff/commen
ts.html
http://spam.example.com/stuff/paid-
links.html
```

```
# Contacted owner of shadyseo.com on
7/1/2012 to
# ask for link removal but got no
response
domain:shadyseo.com
```

You'll notice a couple things. Firstly the comments are preceded with a # mark, which indicates to the disavow tool that this isn't a link but a comment.

The next thing you'll notice is that you can use domain:example.com to request removal of *all* links on example.com. This is advisable in most cases, and we usually request domain-wide removal of links for all the sites we've identified as spammy.

How long does the disavow process take? Once your text file has been submitted through the disavow tool, it needs to be processed by Google. This can take as long as they like. Once it has been processed, the changes need to be incorporated into the search results, which takes anything from a couple of weeks to a year. Let's take a look at some of our penalty recovery case studies to see what sort of results are possible, and the timescales involved.

Penalty Recover Case Studies

In the following case studies we'll look at some recent examples of sites that have been hit by manual and algorithmic penalties, and how we were able to recover their rankings. It's worth noting that in all cases we were building good quality inbound links throughout the penalty recovery process, as once the penalty is lifted improvements are only seen if Google sees enough good quality inbound links to justify ranking the site prominently.

One of the main mistakes made in DIY penalty recovery is assuming that full ranking will return once the penalty is lifted. However it's the spammy links that once provided good ranking that have been removed, so having disavowed them we can't expect them to provide positive effect anymore. This job is down to good quality links from reputable sites, which is why we recommend that every site engages in high quality link building.

Penalty Recovery Case Study 1 - Penguin

This site suffered from the original Penguin update in 2012. The site owner contacted us in late-2013 as the business had taken a nosedive as a result of the ranking drops. We tweaked some layout elements on the site because they were likely appearing spammy to Google (they had a lot of ads above the fold on the homepage, for example), but their backlink profile was also very spammy having worked with low quality SEO companies for many years. We began an extensive link removal campaign in September, submitting a disavow file with the remaining links in October.

We continued building good quality links using promotional videos, SEO PR and social media throughout, but rankings remained pretty stable. In July we got word that Google was to release another Penguin update (Penguin 3.0) sometime in September - October and we prepared another disavow file to take into consideration any old low quality links that Google had indexed since the first disavow file.

When Penguin 3.0 hit on 16th October, the site saw huge ranking improvements and as the good quality links continued to be indexed, ranking continued improving. At the time of writing the business is back on track and traffic has recovered.

Penalty Recover Case Study 2 - Penguin & Manual Penalties

This site had engaged in a lot of low quality link building and desperately needed a new website. We built a new website for them in the tail end of 2013 which was better optimised, but the rankings only improved slightly. Subsequently we removed as many low quality links as we could and submitted the first disavow file at the end of 2013. As we built more good quality links the site continued to improve in ranking, but to nowhere near the level it maintained during the days when they were spamming heavily.

In May, something very interesting happened. One of the client's IT team had a virus on their computer, which gave hackers access to their website. Google spotted the hack and gave us a message in Webmaster Tools, which we addressed within a matter of hours. We then submitted a reconsideration request mentioning that the hack had been fixed, to show Google that the site could be trusted again. But while we had the option to submit a reconsideration request, we decided to mention the disavow and link removal work we'd done. We hadn't had a manual penalty notification, so technically there was nothing to reconsider, but we suspected that there could be something going on that Google wasn't telling us about. So we listed everything - from contact requests to website owners, removing some onsite over-optimisation, the disavow file linked to in a Google doc link - we outlined it ALL.

We submitted the reconsideration request in early June in early August we received a message in Webmaster Tools saying that a manual spam action had been lifted. Bear in mind that there had been NO notification of a manual action, but as we'd felt the rankings weren't responding as we expected, we decided to submit a reconsideration request anyway. The notification from Google showed that actually there *had* been a manual action applied. It's the only time we've seen it happen and we haven't seen it since, which just shows that when it comes to ranking recovery you've got to use every tool available and, of course, never give up.

Once this manual action was lifted, the site saw a significant boost in ranking. In the illustration below, the manual action recovery looks small only when compared to the recovery that happened in October when Penguin 3.0 took the disavow file fully into account and the power of the good quality links we had been building really made their mark. Ranking just exploded and the site is now as prominent as it was during their spamming days.

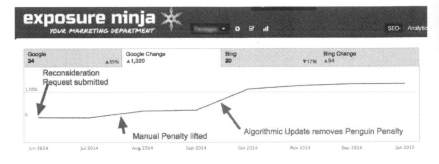

Penalty Recovery Case Study 3 - Fast Recovery Algorithmic Penalty

This site had seen good improvements as a result of good quality links and there was no reason to believe the site was suffering from any penalties, despite a small amount of low quality link building that they had done in the past.

Then in October, the site was hit by Penguin 3.0 and saw a dramatic loss in ranking. We compiled a disavow file immediately and submitted it, and in December the site had not only recovered to the level it had before the penalty, but saw an improvement. Again, this shows that penalisation from low quality links doesn't have to be massive because the effects of the original penalisation were so slightly that neither the site owner nor us had any reason to believe that the site was originally suffering a penalty.

Penalty Recovery Case Study 4 - Fast Recovery Algorithmic Penalty

In this case, the site's backlink profile was almost entirely spam and it was almost invisible in Google results for their main target phrases. We started by creating some good quality links to improve the balance between good and evil. We submitted the first disavow file in August and were expecting the site to see a large improvement at the next algorithm update. When it came, the site saw only a minor improvement though. So we submitted a disavow file that cast a wider net, including sites that were borderline spammy. The following month the site saw a large improvement, demonstrating that if you don't get the result you want - just keep going!

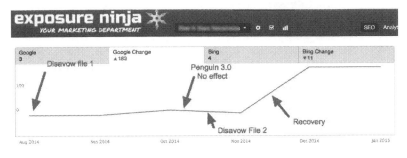

Further Help With Penalty Recovery

If you are suffering from any sort of penalty and would like some help and advice about what to do, we're here to help and can suggest the best course of action. It can be a very stressful time for site owners who have lost a significant amount of ranking, particularly if they came to rely on this ranking for new customers. The downside of good Google rank is that it can outperform all other marketing, leading to marketing complacence and over-reliance on Google rank. Then one day you wake up and it's all gone.

The important thing is not to panic or let despair set in. You *can* recover from this and it's not the end of the world. By removing the junk links, sorting out your website (if necessary), getting some good quality links in place and steering clear of low-quality SEO in future, you'll be back on your feet eventually. We're here to help, whether it's advice, link removal or just reassurance. Drop us an email through the Exposure Ninja website and we'll do what we can.

Social Media

Social media has taken the world by storm, and the possibilities of Twitter, Facebook, Instagram, Pinterest, YouTube and the like can seem to be endless. But it can also be a useful tool to help boost your site's ranking.

Google uses various social signals as ranking factors, whether it's judging the authority of a business or detecting viral content, and popular social channels with plenty of interaction can be a significant asset. Whether it's the number of Google +1s a particular page has (cited by Moz's Ranking Factors study as one of the top ranking factors http://moz.com/search-ranking-factors), or the ratio of Twitter follows to followers, social media is such an important signal as to what is popular online that Google has no choice but to build it into the search algorithms.

What many businesses do is set up a Facebook and Twitter profile, and link these to their websites with all the intention in the world of using them. But life gets in the way and after a short but concerted period of use the posting frequency tends towards zero and social media tumbleweed is spotted blowing across the profiles. As an SEO recommendation they seemed like a good idea at the time, but in reality the business owner ends up being the one responsible for updating their profile and the important tasks involved in running the business inevitably get in the way.

Whether you choose to use social media should depend on the following criteria:

- Whether your competitors use it. If they do and are active, then it's a good idea for you to join them in the world of status updates and tweeting. In all likelihood, they wouldn't be doing it if it wasn't paying or creating some sort of return.
- Whether or not your customers use it, and whether they will value interacting with you. For example, almost everyone uses washing detergent, but how many want hourly tweets about washing detergent from the manufacturer clogging up their timelines? On the other hand, the local plumber who regularly posts money saving tips, examples of great bathroom design, boiler maintenance tips and special seasonal discounts etc. might be extremely interesting to, say, landlords who use social media, and these folks might be likely customers.
- Whether you will actually *use* it. If you know straight away that you won't, there's little point bothering. There's nothing that's more of a turnoff than out of date content and unused social media profiles.
- Whether you are *already* being talked about on social media. Some companies need to check Twitter more often. People have no hesitation about complaining over social media, and if they receive a substandard service their followers could be hearing about it for a long time to come. If your company becomes infamous on Twitter, the

167

best course of action is to get on there and try to rectify the situation rather than ignore it.

- Many larger corporations understand the importance of negative word of mouth and have dedicated teams of people on twitter finding and solving customer problems when they happen, and before the dissatisfaction can spread or get worse. I remember back in 2009 complaining about the service I was getting from a certain British telecoms company. While I was trying to navigate my way through seemingly endless automated menu options to speak to someone extremely unhelpful in India or another popular call centre destination, I tweeted my fury. To my utter shock and amazement, I got a reply from their official account asking for my customer details so they could get the problem fixed. I replied and within minutes they had tracked down the source of our slow line. Meanwhile, I was still on hold on the phone.

If your website covers a market that people are really passionate about (fashion, food, motorbikes, cameras or photography, for example) it's a good idea to force yourself to use social media whether or not any of your competitors use it. There is an unbelievable hunger out there for up-to-date content around subjects for which people are passionate, and if you can position yourself as an expert in your category with some interesting, insightful and informative tweets or status updates, you will

168

generate quite a following and this can be a huge asset in terms of sales and visits to your site.

Social Media and Links

We're often asked what sort of strategy businesses starting on Social Media should use to maximise the SEO benefits. Firstly, our advice for most companies is to use your blog as your online 'content hub'. Any posts that you write, articles you create, videos you make etc. should be kept on your blog with your social media pages then linking to that blog post. This way, you have links pointing at your site and if your content gets liked or shared, it's *your* website rather than Mark Zuckerberg's which gets the link juice.

Secondly, post content that is actually likely to get these shares. If you can find a viral angle in your content that gets a good response from your customers that'll be great for business and even better for your SEO.

Thirdly build an audience. The most common 'audience killing' mistake that most DIY social media marketers fall victim to is posting exclusively promotional posts. Posting links to your website every 3 hours won't increase your traffic or audience if there isn't a compelling benefit for your audience in the content. Make everything you post interesting or entertaining, preferably both. If you're posting boring self-promotional content then expect not to grow your audience or attract any links. And don't forget that you don't have to create all of your social media content yourself - you can retweet or repost popular content from elsewhere too.

Using Videos to Leapfrog Pages and Pages of Your Competitors

As you've probably noticed, Google sometimes includes videos in its search results. These videos tend to get a disproportionately high number of clicks, and can be a great way to secure multiple listings on the front page. Better yet, your competitors are almost certainly not using video in this way, making competition much softer. In fact, showing up with a video can be one of the quickest ways to leapfrog onto the front page, and if you are the only video on the front page you will stand out like a Lamborghini in a scrap heap. The beautiful thing is that your website doesn't have to be *anywhere near* the front page of Google for your video to get to the front page.

Lots of people automatically disregard making videos because they think they'll be really expensive, time consuming and they don't really know where to start. But actually there are plenty of shortcuts that mean you could have a decent promo video online within 30 minutes, without a camera or any fancy software.

Rather than being big expensive productions, there are plenty of companies who provide short promotional video tools online and within a couple minutes you can have a promotional video for your website. Head over to www.Get2TheTopOfGoogle.com/offers for my recommendations.

171

Sites like Animoto and Nawmal allow you to create promotional videos online, which you can download and reupload it to YouTube and every other video site that you can find. It's a good idea to target the video at your main target keywords and use them as the title. In the description add some keyword-rich words about your website and a link to the relevant page on your site, as well as a transcription of the video if you can, as this gives Google the content in a readable format.

The best video websites we've found for uploading your videos to get them on the front page are:
- Dailymotion (paid)
- Viddler
- Metacafe
- YouTube
- Photobucket

If your videos are well optimised with good titles, descriptions and channel info, you can sometimes get multiple instances of the same video showing up on the front page. I currently have 3 videos in the top 4 Google results for one of our clients, with the same video on YouTube, Dailymotion and Metacafe. The main website is ranking on the first page as well, but it's the videos that grab people's attention!

Of course, you'll also want to embed your videos on your website because not only will it catch the eye of your website visitors, but Google likes videos too. Using videos with optimised titles and descriptions also further establishes the relevance of your website for your chosen keywords. Sites with rich media (videos, pictures, embedded social media) tend to rank better, so it's a good idea to include your videos on the site on product/service pages, in the blog and anywhere else that you can get your message across in video form.

Your Strategy

How to Plan An Unstoppable Google Strategy

So now you have all the tools at your disposal to plan and implement a killer SEO plan. In this section I will help you sketch out something that works for you and then get to work implementing it.

Initial Research

The research you do into your market and competitors is absolutely key. In order to beat your competition you need to know their strengths, weaknesses and where to exploit them. You also need as good an understanding as anyone about your customers' habits online so you can meet them where they are.

The first step is simply searching for your product or service and seeing what comes up. As we discussed in the competitor analysis sections, make a note of your competitors, who is showing up, where, and what they are showing up with (titles and descriptions in the Google results). See how the results change if you search for a variation on your main term – is it the same few websites at the top of Google for each variation and different product or service category or are all the searches dominated by one or more players?

Next you'll be studying your competitors' websites and noticing the following:

- Which keywords do they seem to be targeting, and how often do they use them on the page? Do they know which keywords they should be targeting?
- How much text is on their pages?
- What are the pages on their site called?
  o Do they use different pages for each product or service, or is everything on one page?
- How is the website structured?
- Are there a lot of pages all linked from the homepage, or do you go through different levels of pages to find more and more specialized content?
- Are they using social media?
- What do their Meta Description, Title tags and Meta Keywords say? (Find these by right clicking on an empty area of the page and clicking 'View Source')
- How big is the site?
  o Are there a lot of pages?

Remember that the goal at this stage is just to absorb what your competition are doing and make a note of anything that particularly stands out, surprises you or that is significantly different to your website. You'll also want to jot down any keywords that you hadn't thought of. Spend time soaking it all up so that when you come to planning your own strategy you already have a good understanding of what you're going up against.

Keyword Research (Keyword Planner)

The next step in your plan to dominate Google is to head over to the Keyword Planner and start formulating a list of suitable target keywords. Use the process outlined in the Keyword Planner section earlier in this book to identify your short/medium and long-term target keywords according to search volume, competition and commercial intent. Bear in mind that your target keywords will likely change over time as you adapt to the feedback that your market gives you, so in reality your keyword list will be constantly evolving.

If you're already running a well-managed Adwords campaign you can use data from this to inform your keyword selection too. Notice which keywords and ads are bringing the most clicks, impressions and (if you're tracking them) conversions. If you have real life data and a proven conversion funnel, this is where you should start. If not, then Google Keyword Planner data will do nicely.

The next stage of your plan is to sketch out your website's structure, whether or not you plan to change it. If you don't have control over your own website and it is not currently ranking well on Google, this is the best time to decide to go it alone and take responsibility for building your own site or have a site built that you *can* get into and make necessary changes. It can be far quicker to start from scratch than negotiate with web designers who don't understand SEO, not to mention that an invisible website is costing you a lot more money in lost business than a highly-visible one would cost to be developed. Sometimes it's a hard decision, particularly if funds are tight, but looking back you'll see it as one of the best business decisions you'll make.

You know by now that I love Wordpress and almost all the sites my companies build for our clients are Wordpress because it gives you complete control over the content, layout and structure in a simple and non-technical way. If you're technically competent, you might want to have a go at building your own Wordpress site and we have some help available in the form of our video course *Wordpress Mastery Made Simple*.

When sketching out your website structure, you will want to decide on your top level pages (Home, Products/Services, About, Contact) and then any second level pages will need to branch off these top level pages. These second level pages should be built with general keywords in mind (e.g. Ladies Hair, Gents Hair; Wedding Dresses, Ball Gowns; Sports Cars, Saloons). Then decide on third level pages to branch off these second level pages. These third level pages should be targeted at specific keywords or phrases (Popular ladies hairstyles, smart ladies hairstyles; Corset top wedding dresses, Satin wedding dresses; Cabriolets, 2-Seaters).

The aim is to have your website structure neatly organized and easy for your website's visitors to quickly find the information most relevant to them.

URLs and Links

It's also important to have well-optimized page titles on your website. Using easy-to-understand titles that contain the keyword the page is designed for can get you a great head start in the rankings.

Using 'pretty' links like www.mattthebuilder.com/home-extensions is far better than www.mattthebuilder.com/?id=321 for both search engines and real people.

The domain you choose for your website is an important decision too. Although it can seem logical to use your business name, this isn't always what potential customers will be searching for. It can be a good idea to use a descriptive name (and include your location if you're a local business) in your URL.

Remember that you can always point additional domains at your website using 301 redirects if you have a base of existing links pointing at another domain which you'd like to bring over to the new, better one.

Planning and Writing

Next comes the planning and writing of the content for your website's pages. Remember to write with your keywords in mind, but not to sacrifice readability or usefulness to the humans who will be reading your pages. A website at the top of Google is useless (and won't stay top for long) if people don't find it useful and interesting.

Write in a friendly and personal style as If you were having a conversation with your reader and remember to include your keywords and variations as well as plenty of mentions of your location if you're a local business.
It's also a good idea to include the main keyword each of your pages target in the heading (h1).

With any pictures used on the page, include your keyword as the Alt text, and write descriptions/captions if they are relevant.

You can also include internal links between your pages to direct people from one page to another from inside the text. An example of a good use of internal links might be linking to a specific product or service page or linking to your contact page each time you write Contact Us.

Research shows that Google takes notice of the text used in internal links, so be sure to use the keywords each page is targeted at in any links you make, for example `<a href="http://mattthebuilder.com/single-storey-extensions">Single Storey Extensions</a>`, where 'Single Storey Extensions' is the anchor text (and target keyword).

Promoting Your Site

Once your site is built, it's time to promote it like crazy. Google loves backlinks and by using www.ahrefs.com or www.backlinkwatch.com you can find out how many backlinks your competitors have, and also where they come from.

You'll usually find that plenty of them come from directories and forums, and you can add these to your list of websites to target to get backlinks. Submitting your website to good quality directories is a great place to start collecting plenty of backlinks and there are literally thousands of directories out there from general directories of all websites, to specific local directories and specialist directories targeting a particular market or niche.

Be sure to complete your directory listings as fully as possible in order to make your entry stand out and get any preferential treatment that the directory might give to listings with high completion percentages. Including a website link is critical, and if you are a local business registered with Google+ it's a good idea to include your name, phone number and address exactly as it is shown on your Google+ listing as this will give it more weight and help to boost its ranking.

For the next phase of your promotion, it's a good idea to explore SEO/PR. In almost every niche there are magazines and sites that collect well-written articles and blog posts to be a useful source of information. Whether it's a respected industry news site, an online magazine or simply a prominent blogger or commentator, these sites will often be glad for good quality expert-written content that would be useful to their readers. In return you get a juicy backlink to your site from an authority in your market.

When approaching journalists or editors for an article it's important to play up on your expertise in the industry. Remember that good quality magazines will never publish low quality writing stuffed full of keywords, so if you approach them and they lay down a stringent set of requirements that's usually a good sign that the site will remain a high quality authority in future, thus making it more desirable.

In the pitch we usually offer a few suggestions of subjects that we could cover and let the journo or editor choose the most suitable. We also offer them exclusivity on the article meaning that it doesn't fall foul of Google's duplicate content flags and the magazine gets a story that their competitors don't.

At the end of your article it's a good idea to include a short bio section where you link to your Website and Google+ pages, as well as Twitter and Facebook profiles if relevant. In addition to including a link to your own website in the bio section, we also tend to include 'deep' links in the body of the article because they holds more weight with Google and gives a more natural link profile.

News and press releases are another great way to generate links and promote your site, and local news websites can be a fantastic place to get news articles published, particularly if you are a local business, as they are usually pressed for stories. If you can offer them a well-written story about something that will be of interest to their readers, you have done all the hard work for them.

They also tend to be more likely to let you mention and link to your website more often. Try to use anchor text if they'll let you get away with it, but bear in mind that they will probably strip out any code before uploading the article to the website.

As for the content of any news or press release article you write, use your imagination! A story about your website might not be interesting enough to justify inclusion, but a story about the latest trends in X or the fashion amongst customers in Y probably will be, and might just be something that the publication wouldn't not be able to cover without your expertise. If the article proves a hit and they like it, don't be afraid to ask for a more regular spot that will give you much more exposure – and importantly, more backlinks! A regular guest blog on a high profile site can do wonders for your profile in that market.

Another great place to promote your website (subtly) is on forums relevant to your subject area. Many forums are extremely tight with their spam policies so might not allow new posters (or anyone for that matter) to post links, but by contributing to the forum over time you can begin to build a relationship with the other forum dwellers and will find natural places to mention your website.

If the forum allows users to put links in their signatures, you have to exploit this opportunity and include a link (with keyword-rich anchor text) in your signature. Quite often, specialist forums will have a decent page rank so can be a great source of quality backlinks. Be aware that this strategy has been spammed to death so these links give far less benefit than they used to, and forums that have been heavily spammed (they usually have no manual approval process for new members) are best avoided.

This is one of those promotion strategies that not only helps your website out by building your Google listing, but can also drive targeted, quality traffic to your website. Be helpful, answer questions and give honest advice to people in your industry and you *will* get noticed.

Google+ Setup and Integration

Next, you'll want to set up and/or optimise your Google+ page. Start with your personal page and remember to add your website address to the list of links that you contribute to.

Once your personal profile is ready, you'll want to set up a Google+ page for the website or business itself. In Google+ go to Pages then click to set up a page. Choose the right category (e.g. local place or business) and fill in as much of the info as you can. Remember to include pictures, description, hours of business as well as adding your website address. Add a link back to the Google+ page from your website too, so people that want to leave a review can do easily.

If your business has a physical address and this is relevant (i.e. you are a local business and want to show up in map results) you'll need to verify your business by asking Google to send you a postcard at your address. Once your page is verified, you will be eligible to show up with an address block in the search results. More information about this is available in my Google+ Local guide.

On-going Promotion

Google likes to see a steady stream of promotion for your website and SEO isn't really something that you can 'set and forget', so my advice would be to set aside at least half an hour per week to promote your website online in as many targeted places you can find.

Once you have run out of forums and directories relevant to your area, you can try asking suppliers, customers and other local/relevant websites to link to you and you might be surprised how many people will agree if you just ask.

Also remember to update your website as often as you can by adding new content. A great way to make this really easy is to start a blog on your site. Here you can write about anything that interests you that will also be of value to your customers. It's never easy to start, but once you've started your blog you'll find it much easier to get into the swing of things. Google loves websites that are updated frequently, and the more frequently your website is updated, the more often Google's spiders will crawl and index it.

If you run Twitter and Facebook pages, remember to tweet or link to your latest blog posts as this helps to increase the number of links to your website as well as directing a good flow of visitors. You can interact with other people in your industry and report interesting news to boost your credibility and authority. In my opinion credibility and authority will become an increasingly important element of SEO as we move beyond an anonymous web to one where the author of a particular site, post or article has an effect on its ranking.

If you have implemented the testimonial rich text snippets, you'll also want to keep these as up-to-date as possible. The date of the most recent testimonial will show up in the Google search results and we know from experimentation that searchers will be more likely to click on sites that have been updated most recently.

Further Help and Information

I'd like to thank you for reading this guide and I sincerely hope that it has been useful to you. A lot of website owners pay good money to have these strategies implemented for them, and I think it's important that you understand exactly what it takes to get to the top of Google, because it is so important.

Hopefully you can see that while it's not *easy* to rank number 1, and some markets are certainly tougher than others – for example banking, mortgages or anything where you are competing with £50,000+ per month SEO teams – the tasks involved are actually relatively simple and a large portion of the work is simply building a readable website, making it useful to people and then promoting it.

If, having seen what is involved in getting a website to the top of Google, you have decided that you would like some help with some or all of your SEO work then we'd be happy to talk with you about taking it on so you can get on with running the business. My company Exposure Ninja (http://exposureninja.com) builds websites and provides SEO and online promotion for businesses, whether local, national or international. We're good at what we do and genuinely offer a level of promotion work that is unheard of at our price point.

Throughout this book I have sung the praises of Wordpress as a website building tool and if you are yet to build a website or would like to take control of your own website, I cannot recommend it highly enough. Wordpress is free to use and quite simple once you know your way around, although the initial setup can be a little complicated if you are new to FTP.

I have a course showing you exactly how to setup and maintain a Wordpress site, which is included as part of MarketingU membership: http://marketingu.ninja. You can claim a 20-day free trial by using the code NINJA245

How To Get To The Top Of Google+ Local

Tim Kitchen
www.Get2TheTopOfGoogle.com
www.ExposureNinja.com

Introduction

Why this book exists

In April 2012, the first edition of 'How to Get to The Top of Google' hit the stores and was instantly way more popular than I could have hoped. The feedback was great and it wasn't long before the success stories started coming in.

But by far the biggest request was for more information about Google Places, Google Maps, Google+ Local and the various names and products Google uses to try to capture and present information about our local area. Everyone from car mechanics to electricians, musicians and florists wanted to know how to show up on that map on the front page of Google. So I realized I needed to answer this question.

What Google+ Means for Local Businesses

For marketers and owners of local businesses, Google+ is one of the biggest opportunities to attract new customers since Google's dominance of the search engine world began.

It's still not uncommon to see unclaimed or poorly optimised Google+ listings with great placement at the top of the page, listed above well-optimised and heavily back linked *regular* websites, which are shown further down the page. Worse still, some local businesses found their websites had been bumped onto page 2 as a result of the increase in the number of map results shown on the Search Engine Results Page (SERP). Sometimes there are as few as 3 regular listings on a page because of the number of map results, and on mobile devices these map listings are given even more importance so it's easy to see why they attract so much attention from businesses eager to boost their exposure online.

The truth is that getting to the top of Google+ Map listings can be a phenomenal shortcut and alternative to more traditional SEO and competing with well-optimised and professional websites.

With their map listings, Google is attempting to cement their service as the 'go to' destination for people who need the services of a local business. By showing phone numbers and addresses for the +Local results, customers who are quickly looking for contact or location info aren't required to click through to the business website.

This is all part of Google's plan. As we've seen with Google images, stock prices, translations, definitions, exchange rates and many other set definable requests ("$48 in £" or "weather today in Bristol" for example), Google is gradually adopting a new role: rather than simply gathering data it thinks might be relevant, it's beginning to make choices and dig a little deeper in order to provide the exact information required direct to the searcher, without them even having to visit the website originally providing that information. The future of search is about answering questions directly rather than just presenting a list of possible sources of answers.

This shift away from simply providing a list of websites that might be of interest, to actually giving the searcher the information they require might seem subtle at first, but its impact on the web is yet to be fully realized.

As many local business owners are coming to understand, having a good well optimised website is no longer enough in many markets. Playing by Google's rules and jumping through their hoops is more important than ever, and Google Places and +Local is the latest hoop smart business owners are crowding to jump through.

Google Places vs. Google+ for Business vs. Google+ Local vs. Google Maps. Now Google My Business?

The naming and organization of Google's various local products has been a total mess since about 2010. No one outside professional marketing agencies really knows their way around Google+ for business, and even we struggle with the frequent updates to naming, layout and function.

Part of the problem is that Google has had to auto generate a lot of business listings whilst others have signed up to various services over the years, and each time Google 'upgrades' its offering, they're hesitant to roll out the new look to everyone for fear of destroying millions of pages that businesses already feel a sense of ownership over. So the roll out is slow and painful and any map listing can contain 3 or more generations of Google+ pages, giving a total lack of continuity.

In 2014 *Google My Business* was unveiled as a way for business owners to keep on top of their Google services. The idea is that you have to log in to only one site to get your Google+ Business and Google Analytics dashboards. It was supposed to make Google+ more accessible for businesses, but in reality it's no simpler and take up will be extremely low amongst business owners themselves.

For *consumers,* Google+ Local is the product they use to find local businesses, read reviews and do all they used to do in Google Places, but confusingly they are often seeing Google Places results that have been upgraded to Google+ Local.

Added to that, if you are a Google+ user who also owns a business, you can set up a Google+ for Business page. As the name would suggest, this is a Google+ page specifically for your business. It also contains local information and over time Google will be merging + for Business and + Local pages into one.

Google Maps is still Google Maps. The results that show up in Google Maps results and on the front page of Google in the map results and 7-pack are Google+ Local results *and* Places results that look like +Local results.

If this sounds confusing, it is. Sorry.

In the interests of clarity and being as future proof as possible, for the majority of the rest of this guide I will refer only to Google+ Local, which encompasses all of the local business Google+ functionality that gets your business showing up on the map.

With all that cleared up (...) let's get stuck in!

How to Look at Google+ Local

The truth is that the local results that Google displays are just another type of search result. Because of this, many of the standard SEO (Search Engine Optimisation, or 'trying to improve ranking') best practices apply, albeit with small modifications.

So in order to transfer our understanding of regular SEO to best understand exactly what's going on with Google+ Local, we need a framework. Think of this framework as the language dictionary that helps us translate best practice from regular SEO to our new language of Google+ Local.

Regular Google Results

So first let's look at the most commonly accepted 'rules' of regular Search Engine Optimisation. It's worth noting that while each of the following are important, it is not always necessary to have *all* of these factors highly optimised in order to get great results.

1. Keyword matching. It's obvious that when you search for "New Cars Croydon", Google is going to be returning websites that it considers relevant for the phrase (and individual words) "new cars Croydon". These

words known as 'keywords' have always been the foundation of Google's search. Keywords can be used in different places to serve different purposes, for example:

i.   In the website's title. This is a great place to start and makes it obvious for Google what the webpage's content is focused on. A page called 'New Cars in Croydon' is likely to be pretty well targeted to our "new cars Croydon" searcher.

ii. In the content of the web page. Again, when Google is crawling the webpage, the more instances of the keyword it finds, the safer it is to assume that the page will be of interest to someone searching that particular phrase.

iii. In the content on the pages linking to your site, whether from other websites or from different places on your own website. Links from websites covering relevant topics hold much more weight than general sites, as do links from high authority sites.

2. Back linking. In order for Google to show searchers the most relevant results possible, it likes to know which websites are the most popular. That way it can be sure that when you type in "Wal Mart" you get the Wal Mart website rather than a forum discussing Wal Mart. Although the Wal Mart forum might have more mentions of the phrase "wal mart" than the Wal Mart homepage, it is not as popular a page as the retail giant's own. One of the ways Google measures popularity is by seeing how many times each page is mentioned or linked to by other

pages on the Internet. These links are known as backlinks. What's more is that Google gives each website a popularity score, known as PageRank. In Google's eyes, a link from a high PageRank (more important) website is worth more than a link from a low PageRank (less important) website. Think of it like this: if all the cool kids are talking about you, you *must* be cool too.

3.   The structure and size of the website. Another important factor is that your website *works*. That is there are no broken pages and it's not just a simple one-page job but has plenty of content for interested searchers to quench their thirst. Remember that Google is simply doing its best to try and imitate human preferences. When you are looking for some information, you are likely to be more impressed by a website that has lots of relevant info compared to a site that has a few lines of information stuffed full of the keyword and offering nothing original. The Google bots also need to be able to 'crawl' your website and find their way around, so making sure that you have simple navigation is a good idea. People should be able to find the information they want from your site within a couple of clicks at most, and it should be intuitive where to look.

4.   Time on site and bounce rate. When Google shows your website in the results page, it's taking a gamble: "will this person be grateful to me for showing them this website? Or will

they leave dissatisfied and go over to Bing?"
Google wants to know that its searchers are
valuing the results it's serving up. One of the
ways it judges this is by measuring the time
visitors spend on your site, and the number
that immediately 'bounce back' to the
Google results page. On the whole,
spending a short time on the website is a
sign that it wasn't very interesting, useful or
relevant, and Google will want to know this
information. The best way to keep visitors on
your website immediately with very little
effort is to put up a short video. The video
can be 30 seconds long and could just be a
quick promo video made on animoto
(www.animoto.com) or another similar site.
The point is that once a visitor clicks on your
site and sees a video, they're likely to watch
it. If the video is 1 minute long, you have just
increased the average time on your site by 1
minute for everyone who watches the video

So those are the basics behind regular SEO.

How Google+ Local and Regular Google Results Fit Together

Our experience setting up and running around
200 local websites for clients in different
industries is this: the best results come when you
do *both* regular SEO and Google+ Local
optimisation.

If you do *only* regular SEO, then even if your website ranks highly, it could still be stuck at the bottom of the page below the local results. At the same time, if you only set up a Google+ Local page and skip having your own website, not only will you find it harder to rank on the maps results but you'll also find it *much* harder to convert local traffic into customers. In my experience, visitors still want to see a website. Just having your name and number show up at the top of Google is not enough – surfers want information about you before they pick up the phone. With the amount of choice online, you really need to be showing your best in order to get their business.

Ideal Results

So the approach I'm going to prescribe in this guide is a hybrid of regular SEO and Google+ Local Optimisation and promotion.

It's the approach that has got our clients and me numerous first place listings in both +Local results and also the +Local/website hybrid results. These hybrid results are my favourite because they really dominate a page: as well as your regular website listing, a pin and address block is visible which can also be seen on the map.

I've included a screenshot of what I mean below:

As you can see, this 'super listing' is the result of
a combination SEO and +Local approach which
gives the website great position but also adds
the local element.

(In case you're wondering about the effect of this
sort of result, this listing has literally changed the
site owner's life. To see the testimonial, head
over to http://exposureninja.com).

The sort of result above requires a lot of time
and patience. The work for this listing took about
6 months for the +Local integration started to be
visible.

Although I recommend a solid SEO campaign to
go alongside a Google+ Local/Google Places
campaign, this book will focus on only the local
element. The regular SEO side is covered by my
book "How to Get to the Top of Google",
available on Amazon or through
http://get2thetopofgoogle.com

Google+ Local – First Steps

Your Personal Google+ Page

The first step to take is to sign up for Google+. Before setting up or claiming a business page, I'd recommend setting up a personal profile. Head over to http://plus.google.com and click the SIGN UP button. If you already have a Google account, you can instead just sign in with your regular username and password and you will be guided through the process of upgrading your profile to Google+.

As mentioned in my book 'How to Get to the Top of Google', there are advantages to being on Google+ from an SEO point of view, and little tricks like using authorship markup can be really powerful in boosting your website's visibility. But that side of things is covered in more detail in that book and we are primarily concerned with the local element here so simply fill out your profile as completely as possible, adding pictures, descriptions, links… the whole works.

Creating Your Google+ Local Page

Once your personal Google+ profile is complete, on the left hand side of the page you'll see a menu. Expand it then click the Pages option.

Next, click the link to Create New Page and choose the relevant category. If you're a local business (a pretty safe bet considering the subject of this book!), then the first option 'Local Business or Place' is the one to choose.

You will now be asked to enter your primary phone number, as this is how Google identifies if you already have a listing set up (whether someone did it manually or it was automatically created as a Places listing). Remember that the goal is to find existing listings if they exist – we don't want to create duplicate listings if we can at all help it, trust me!

Once you enter your phone number, Google will present you with any businesses that match. If there are no matches, you will be taken through to enter your address and the details of your business. If you find that your business *is* already listed, you can click to confirm the address and category before clicking to create the page.

How is my business already listed?

When Google was building its Google Places product, it scraped business information from numerous places in order to create listings for many local businesses automatically. Then once Google Places became Google+ Local, these listings were upgraded to the new format. The result is that many businesses already have Google+ Local listings, even if they didn't manually add them.

Google has been known to punish duplicate listings, so best to stay on the safe side.

The Phone Number and Google+ Local

It's worth stopping for a moment to talk about the role of the phone number in the world of Google+ Local.

What we've actually *just seen* is a pretty significant insight, I believe, into the workings of Google+ Local and there are some significant implications for ranking.

We've just seen how Google identifies a business by its phone number (particularly local landline numbers). There was no request for address, website or even business name. All that was required was a phone number. This makes sense if you consider that many businesses don't have websites, some will share names and often one building will house many businesses. But phone numbers are nearly always unique to the business.

I've long held the view that a phone number is to Google+ Local what a website address is to regular Google search algorithms. It's a unique identifier for your business. In other words the phone number is the thing you promote, the thing you get listed, the thing that Google looks at to judge popularity.

This is where our experience of regular SEO and +Local SEO really starts to converge: the strategy we use for our clients is to promote their Google+ Local listing in the same way as we promote their websites. But rather than use a web address to link, we'll use a 'citation'. Citations are basically a listing of a business's name, address and phone number. I personally believe the phone number is responsible for nearly all of the effect, but it does no harm to include the whole citation. We'll look at citations in more detail later on, but for now let's continue setting up your Google+ profile.

Profile Basics

As with everything Google+ you'll want to fill in the details of your profile as completely as possible, and that includes adding a profile photo. Unlike your personal Google+ page, this doesn't necessarily have to be a head shot of you and should be a logo, picture of your premises or something else relevant. If you don't have a suitable picture just yet you can add one later, but it is advisable to add one.

You'll be offered the choice to promote your page on your personal Google+ profile and this is optional.

The next step is to start filling in the publicly visible information. You'll see a button at the top of the screen to Edit Profile and this will allow you to write an introduction, put in your hours of business, add additional phone numbers, link to your website and also put in some other links of interest. This can be a good place to link to any promotional videos you have or other sites relevant to your business.

You can also add photos and videos to your page, and this is advisable. Remember that the more complete the profile, the better.

Linking Your Website

If you have a website and have linked to it in your About section, you'll see a button appear to link this website to your Google+ Local page. To do this, all you need to do is click the button, copy the text that appears and have this embedded somewhere on your website's homepage. This step is absolutely crucial because it's what allows Google to verify that the website and Google+ Local page are associated so that they can display the Google+ Local information alongside the website in search results, as seen in the example earlier.

To be clear, linking your website to your Google+ Local page doesn't *guarantee* that Google will show address information next to your website in the search results, it just makes it possible.

Unfortunately Google likes to take its time in approving such linking, but nevertheless this is one of the most important steps to take in boosting your Google+ Local visibility.

Verifying Your Google+ Local Listing

The next step is also crucial for ensuring that you are visible in local searches. You'll notice that your Google+ Local page is labelled 'Unverified'. This means that Google hasn't seen verification that you, the person responsible for editing the page, are in actual fact the business owner.

In order to verify the page, Google needs to confirm your address. By clicking the button Verify Now, you can ask Google to send a postcard through to your business address containing a PIN number. Once you get this postcard, you can head back to your Google+ Local page and type it in to verify your listing.

The postcard usually takes around 10 days to arrive in the UK. If after a couple weeks it still hasn't arrived, you can request another to be sent out. But this step is really important so I'd recommend not putting it off or ignoring it.

Again, once you've entered your PIN, there will be a wait while Google confirms the verification. How long depends on how Google is feeling, and there's nothing you or I can do about it.

Just as we do for regular SEO, I'm going to break down the components of a successful Google+ Local promotion campaign into 2 categories: on-listing and off-listing.

On-Listing Strategies

Just like Onsite optimisation in regular SEO, on-listing strategies in Google+ Local are things we can do to the listing itself in order to help it rank higher.

Business Name

Your business name should be real. In other words, it should be what you call your business. The temptation might be to stuff your business title with lots of juicy keywords: "Cutting Edge Hair, Hair salon in Chichester, bridal hair, wedding hair, L'Oreal colour specialists" and such spammy junk. Keywords = good, right?

This is frowned upon by the big G who understandably doesn't want to see the +Local results become overrun with keyword spam in the way that regular search results have in the past.

However, what I suggest to many of our clients is that unless they already have established brand awareness in their town, they might consider choosing a more 'optimised' name for their business.

Let's take the local plumber as a typical example. Many plumbers will, without hesitation, call their companies after themselves: Barry White Plumbing & Heating Services. This is fine, but actually unless Barry is well known in the area, there are more suitable names that could get him showing up higher in Google.

If Barry is based in Leicester for example, he might choose to call himself Leicester Plumbing & Heating. This is going to more closely match what people search for, as well as give him a bit more credibility when he does show up in the search results. While it's not advised to add extra keywords to a business name, in some cases you can rename the business to contain keywords. This is perfectly acceptable and has been responsible for some of our clients making a ridiculously large return on investment on our local marketing services.

But I know that it's not always possible. If you're a shop or have an established website already and a sneaky change of name isn't practical, then don't be tempted to add extra keywords in the name field. Don't worry; there are plenty of other things we can do...

Phone and Email

It's obviously important that the phone number on the Google+ Local listing is correct, and where possible this should be a geographic landline because Google can use this to geolocate the business and it is another reassuring sign of a 'genuine' business. For our clients that have multiple offices or want to serve multiple locations, we recommend setting up different regional phone numbers through a service like Voipfone which can all be directed to one number or their mobile.

You can add email addresses to your Google+ Local profile in the Contact Info section where your phone numbers are displayed. Simply choose Email from the dropdown box. Email addresses should, if possible, be from your website's domain, i.e. barry@leicesterplumbingandheating.com rather than sparklefairy69@hotmail.co.uk. Ask yourself 'if Google was trying to see which option represented a more legitimate business, which would they choose?'

Your Google+ Description

The Introduction section on your Google+ Local profile serves 2 purposes:
1. To give visitors an insight into what you do
2. To give Google an insight into what you do.
So you want to make sure that you're primary keywords are included in this introduction, but try to include them in a classy, refined way rather than sounding spammy or unnatural. It's worth mentioning the areas you serve as well as any variations of your key phrases that describe your product or service.

Don't be afraid of writing a lot of text here, and you can also link to specific pages on your website, for example: "we have a large customer base in Leicester, and our testimonials from past plumbing customers are extremely important to us. Here you included a link with good anchor text as well as your location and service.

Google+ Photos

Adding photos is a very good idea to create a more complete profile that is more likely to convert potential visitors. It also shows Google that you are putting in the effort, and if Google has the choice between showing an incomplete profile and one with loads of photos… you get the idea!

If you're feeling really adventurous you can geotag the photos you upload in Picasa, which will give Google more location information.

Videos in Google+

As with pictures, adding videos to your Google+ profile is a good idea. Unfortunately in Google+ you are actually required to upload videos to the page, whereas before in Google Places you could simply link to them from YouTube.

Google+ Reviews

Reviews: everyone's favourite. For some markets, Google has joined forces with Zagat, a local review service. Zagat has a rather confusing scoring system with a maximum of 30.

The result of this is that a 26 in a red box looks at first glance like a very poor score out of 100, whereas actually it's considered a very *good* score.

For other markets customers are required to review the Google+ page itself while they're logged in to their Google+ account. We've seen a significant ranking benefit to having 5 or more reviews, which also sees an average star rating appear in the Google+ results. Encouraging your customers to review you on Google+ is a VERY GOOD IDEA, but unfortunately your customers will need to sign up to Google+ first, so you might have to help them by giving them instructions.

If you had one, reviews from your old Google Places pages still show up, but without scores and are attributed to the anonymous sounding 'A Google User'.

Reviews used to be aggregated from other sites as well, such as Thomson Local, Qype and others, but whilst you can sometimes still click to see reviews left on other sites, they are no longer automatically displayed on the Google+ Local page and they don't contribute to overall rating. This is a real source of annoyance for businesses that for years focussed on these other platforms to build an excellent base of reviews that are now virtually invisible, whilst their Google+ Local page lies barren and review-less.

The Google +Local review system has been the target for various attempts to manipulate and create false reviews to boost rankings. As a result of this, Google is unable to be so straightforward as to rank local listings in order of best reviews – the system is too open to manipulation. It also tends to be a bit overzealous at removing reviews that it thinks could possibly be unnatural, so be aware that reviews can disappear at any time and there's absolutely nothing that you can do about it. Of course having said that, just do everything that you can to get good reviews and get lots of them.

Rather than signing up with multiple Google+ accounts using VPN software to hide your IP address and writing your own reviews, you can take two approaches:
- Ask your customers to leave you reviews. Many of them won't bother and many of the ones that do will be unable to figure out how to do it.
- Head over to the Internet in search of buying reviews.

I recommend the first approach, but most people who do the second look in the direction of Fiverr and Amazon's Mechanical Turk, which is a platform for recruiting people from around the world to perform small tasks very cheaply. All I'd say about this is that Google isn't stupid, and if anyone is going to figure out the whole 'fake reviews' situation, I'd bet my big shiny drum kit on it being Google. Maybe there will one day be a Google Polar Bear update that targets local listings using fake reviews? But maybe you'll get away with it.

Off-listing factors

Just like regular SEO works on the basis of links to your website URL, local SEO is about citations of your business's phone number and *physical* address. When promoting your Google+ Local website, you should aim to get your name, address and phone number (NAP for short) listed in as many relevant places as possible.

Directories

Just like regular SEO, targeted directories and local websites are a great place to start.

But first a warning about directories: many people new to SEO and +Local optimisation will assume that if a few directories is good, then more must be better. They sign up to every directory site under the sun – even the low quality spammy ones, and a bunch that really aren't relevant to their target market. The problem with this approach is that if you do it enough you can raise flags with Google who sees people appearing on these low quality spammy directories as spammers.

The Holy Grail for directory listings are directories that are curated and an actual human being sorts through the new listings and approves them. Ideally you want your directories to be quite difficult to get into, because that keeps the spammers away. Failing that, at least make sure they have a fairly lengthy sign up process (like Freeindex or Yelp for example).

With that said, let's look at the best sorts of directories to target.

Local Area Directories

The first is local directories in our area. If you Google "<your area> business directory", you will usually find a few local business directories specifically targeted to your area. These are fantastic because they're generally kept quite small and relevant and aren't overrun by spam. They're also a good source of local traffic for your website and +Local listing too, so as well as the citation you are more likely to pick up some potential customers. Google likes them because they are *relevant* due to their local focus.

As with all directory listings, try to complete your entry as fully as possible and include pictures if you can. All of these directory sites want their listings to be as complete as possible and potential customers will be more likely to click on you if they can see pictures. In order to boost your +Local page, you can also link directly to it from each directory listing as well. If the listing allows you to enter more than one website address, as well as your main website link, you can add a link to your +Local page. If the directory doesn't allow more than one link, then you can often add a link in the description and where possible make it a live clickable link.

I also like to include a full NAP citation in the description where possible, shown in the exact format used on the Google+ Local page.

Market Specific Directories

The next category of directories you should target is market-specific directories. To find these, simply search for "<your business type> directory", e.g. "funeral director directory". List yourself in as many of these as possible as long as they are good quality and not filled with spam. After the recent Google updates, it's pretty unlikely that spam-ridden directories will be easily findable, but it's still possible so use your judgement and ask: 'does this look like a quality directory I would trust?'

Again it's good practice to include a link to your Google+ Local page in these directory listings because this it will be highly targeted and relevant as a result of the single business category focus of the directory.

High Quality National Directories

The next category of directories is the good quality national business directories. These are sites like Yelp, Qype, Freeindex, Yell, Thomson

Local and Scoot (which populates the Sun and the Independent - a very high ranking directory!). These directories are amongst those favoured by Google because they generally require some level of approval or have a more complicated signup process (for example, our team based in our office in Cebu, Philippines, is unable to sign up to Yelp – it has to be done manually by me or someone else in the UK).

Recommended Directories (UK)

My current favourites for UK-based businesses are:
www.qype.co.uk
www.yelp.co.uk
www.fyple.co.uk
www.hotfrog.co.uk
http://freeindex.co.uk
www.uksmallbusinessdirectory.co.uk
http://directory.independent.co.uk
http://listings.touchlocal.com
www.smilelocal.com
www.misterwhat.co.uk
www.city-visitor.com
www.brownbook.net
www.thomsonlocal.com
www.ufindus.com
www.yell.com
www.tipped.co.uk

Many of these have international versions too, and if you want to find more here's how: search for your product or service, then go through the

Google results pages identifying all the directories that are showing up. Now you know which are the most authoritative in Google's eyes, you can start listing yourself in them.

As mentioned before – complete these listings as fully as possible. Sometimes verification is required before the listing can be fully completed and it can be tempting to skip the final step if this verification takes a couple days. Don't do it! The difference between a fully complete directory listing and a half-assed 'quick basics' job is probably 10 minutes, max. The best 10 minutes you can spend. Well, maybe not *the* best…

Also remember to link to your Google+ Local page and include a full NAP citation, if the directory allows it.

Other Sources of Citations

Because citations of the business's Name Address and Phone number (NAP) are important for getting great +Local rank, it's worth exploring some other places we can put these citations that Google will index.

If you have a Twitter account, consider adding a citation to your Twitter description. Remember you can also link to your Google+ Local page from your Twitter account, which can be great if your Twitter account is active and you are regularly posting relevant messages that are interesting to your target market.

The same goes for Facebook. Many small businesses set up a local business Facebook page expecting it to drive hundreds of 'viral' customers to their business. OK so that's not going to happen, but at least we can use your Facebook page to drive juicy high quality links and citations at your business. Include your NAP listing in the same format as seen on your Google+ Local page, and add a link to the page itself as well as your main website.

For our local clients, we usually set up a YouTube channel and post a few short, very simple promotional videos. In the description for each of these videos we will add a NAP citation as well as a link back to their website. Then from the channel description we'll add another citation with links to the website and +Local page included in the relevant channel links section.

All of these social citations build up the number of citations Google is likely to index, and make high +Local rank far more likely.

If you can get business partners, suppliers or customers to link to your website from theirs and include a NAP citation, that's another good source of quality links in your arsenal. It's far better than spamming blogs or linking in poor quality directories because (hopefully) their sites will be higher quality and more relevant to your business, market or location.

Guest blogging can be a shortcut to getting in front of a large audience, and whenever you write for another website it's good practice to include a link and NAP citation, not only increasing your rank and number of citations but also increasing the chances that visitors who enjoyed the article will become customers down the line.

It's beyond the scope of this Google+ Local guide to show you how to set up guest blogging relationships, but it is covered in the main How to Get to the Top of Google book.

On-Website Factors

We'll now look at some things you can do on your website itself in order to boost your Google+ Local profile, as well as increase conversions of local visitors.

Google maps on linked website

One of the key issues with local website visitors is trust. People often feel more comfortable using a business that is close to them, because they feel a stronger connection and a safety that if something goes horrendously wrong with their purchase, they can go round and get it fixed.

But even for businesses that aren't close by, knowing that they have a physical location makes them seem far more accountable. And nothing says 'physical location' like a map saying, "We are here"!

To add a map showing your business location, first sign into Google and head over to www.google.com/maps. Now you'll need to find your business on the map (please note that you must have set up your Google+ Local listing already to find your business on this map).

Once you have found your business listing on Google maps (try finding your area, searching for your business name and clicking on the red dot

223

marker if your business isn't yet showing up in the results on the left hand side), click on its map location and you'll see more information pop up. You'll also see a link to 'Save to Map'. Click this and select 'Create a new map' from the drop down box, then hit save. Your new map has then been created and it's time to edit it and make it a little more useful for your website visitors. Click Edit on your map page and you'll get the ability to write a Title and Description. Remember to use your keywords & phrases in these descriptions, but also to make them relevant and useful, as they will be displayed anywhere you embed this new map (like on your website).

Once you are happy with your title and description, click save.

The next step is to get the code for this map so that we can embed it on our website. Obviously this step requires that you have access to the code of your website (and that you have a website). If you don't and would like to, feel free to get in touch with us through www.exposureninja.com.

To get the embed code, simply click the button above Save that looks like chain links. You'll then be shown two pieces of code – one for a link and the second to embed the map. If you like you can customise the map (I usually shrink them down a bit) by clicking the Customise link, and once you are happy you can copy the embed code. You can now paste this code anywhere on your site and your visitors will see your business displayed on a map.

As well as being great for your visitors, you now have another link to your business location specifically in a Google friendly format. Awesome! Crack open a Ben & Jerry's to celebrate - I recommend Peanut Butter Cups.

Links to Your Google+ Local Page

As part of your verification of your Google+ Local page, you will have included a link from your website back to this page. But if, like me, you put this link quite small in the footer of the website, it can also be a good idea to include a larger and more visible link on another page of your site. In the next chapter we will be looking at getting reviews for your business on your +Local page, and once you have some quality reviews it can be beneficial to send website visitors over to your +Local page to have a look at these reviews. For that reason, for business clients that are more active in collecting reviews or who use the Google+ Local pages more often, we'll put a link back to their profile on the Contact or Testimonials page of their website.

On-Site Citations

As well as having lots of juicy NAP citations on directories, social media and other websites, it's a great idea to double check that your location details and phone number are 100% correct and visible on every page of your website. You wouldn't believe the number of local businesses who bury their address – or even forget to include it all together – on their websites, expecting all potential customers to pick up the phone.

If you're technically-minded, the best format for your NAP citations on your website is the hCard format. This is a Google-readable special piece of code that identifies your location information as a sort of virtual business card, and allows Google to display it accordingly in the search results.

I haven't seen Google do anything special with the hCard information yet, although other rich snippet text *is* treated differently, so it's likely that at some point in the future this will happen, or that it's treated differently behind the scenes.

If you're running Wordpress, I recommend the WP Customer Reviews plugin as it allows both the hCard info to be shown on every page of your website as well as displaying your customer reviews in hReview format which can lead to the gold stars showing in your Google results page listings. Very cool (and free). For more info, see my other book How to Get to the Top of Google.

Other Factors

Phone Numbers

When trying to show up in a certain area, it's most desirable (both from a Google point of view and a potential customer's point of view) to have a local phone number. The area code should ideally match your target area, but any landline is better than no landline.

If you are a purely mobile business, then one thing you can do is set up a virtual landline from a website like www.voipfone.com. Services like Voipfone allow you to set up a local phone number with an area code of your choice that you can redirect either to your computer, or to another phone - including mobiles.

If you have a number of regional offices each with their own address and phone number, then I recommend setting up different Google+ Local & Places accounts for each one and using their own local numbers. Not only will this give you more locations visible, but it will also make each listing better optimised and as a result more likely to get great ranking.

Proximity to Location

One inescapable fact is that if you are not based near your target location, it is going to be very difficult for you to rank very highly in the maps results. For example, one of my clients installs bathrooms. Because he lives in a tiny village miles from anywhere, we decided that it would be best to target his nearest big city so we set up a well-optimised website, Places and +Local pages for him. Although he rarely shows up as a map result in local search for that city (because he is located about 20 miles outside it), we optimised his site well enough with regular SEO that he gets fantastic Google rank with his combined website *and* local listing.

So in cases where you are at a disadvantage against your competitors due to your distance from your target market, you might want to focus more intensely on regular SEO.

It used to be that those who were closest to the very centre of the location pin in a particular place stood the best chance of ranking well. Over time we've seen this effect start to dilute slightly (a good thing, as it's a very crude measure of relevance), and now you'll notice that it is not the closest businesses to a particular location that necessarily show up, but the best optimised/most popular/most citations that win. Of course as in the example above, business located far outside a location are still at a disadvantage, but it is no longer necessary to be dead centre in order to rank well.

Age of Listing

While having a mature listing isn't necessarily a guarantee for success, brand new listings will be less likely to rank highly early on. Typically we tell clients to allow 4-6 months before the full effect of Google+ Local/Places work has taken effect. During this time we'll run Adwords ads for them to get some early traffic and get things moving, and make sure that the pages have been verified properly and PINs submitted as soon as we get them.

Duplicate Listings

For those who already have a Google+ listing but it hasn't yet been claimed, the temptation can be to 'start again' and create a new listing from scratch. This is against Google's policies though, and as such is inadvisable. Trust me, if I thought you could get ahead this way I'd be advocating it, but in reality the maturity of your existing listing will be much more useful to you that a duplicate listing which could risk your removal entirely.

For this reason, it's always advisable to try and find any existing listings you have when signing up – even if you have to check alternative phone numbers to find them. If you do accidentally create a duplicate listing, it's best to remove the new one and instead optimise the old one and make sure it is up to scratch.

Summary

As Google continues to improve and enhance its search to take into consideration location, social signals and intent, it will be more and more important to 'play ball' with Google's new products and services. Google+ Local and Places is the current best option for local businesses looking to get exposure with searchers in the local area, and hopefully the contents of this guide will help you get started in this relatively new field.

The key aspects of a successful Google+ Local placement:

- Google+ Local page, well optimised, linked to website and with address verified
- Properly optimised website with location, Google map and hCard address information if possible
- Article writing, guest blogging and having other relevant sites link to yours including a NAP citation as well as your website link
- Publicising your Google+ page and encouraging your customers to leave reviews, as this will improve your conversions and lead to more traffic for your page

I hope you've enjoyed this guide and that you are now able to go forth and put these strategies into place. If you need to get in touch my email is tim@exposureninja.com or alternatively you can

get through to me through our website
http://exposureninja.com

Remember to claim lifetime updates to this book
from www.get2thetopofgoogle.com/offers, grab
your free website review and personalised action
plan from www.exposureninja.com/review and
take a free 20-day trial of MarketingU at
http://marketingu.ninja with your voucher code
NINJA245

Go forth and dominate!

Tim Kitchen

30883195R00129

Printed in Great Britain
by Amazon